AGAINST THE SEA

Against the Sea

TRUE STORIES OF
DISASTER AND SURVIVAL

Ralph Barker

ST. MARTIN'S PRESS
NEW YORK

AFFILIATED PUBLISHERS:
Macmillan & Company, Limited, London –
also at Bombay, Calcutta, Madras and
Melbourne – The Macmillan Company of
Canada, Limited, Toronto

CONTENTS

AUTHOR'S NOTE

All these stories were commissioned at various times by the *Sunday Express*, to whom I am doubly indebted for permission to reproduce them in volume form. R.B.

ILLUSTRATIONS

ACKNOWLEDGEMENTS

The copyright in the photographs is acknowledged as follows:

1 and 7c – Press Association.

3a and 6 – U.P.I.

3b, 4, 7a, 8a, 8b and 8c – London Express News and Feature Services.

5b – J. Smailes & Son, Rhyl.

6 (inset) – Fox Photos.

Personal photographs are gratefully acknowledged to Harry Bell, Ernest Fieldhouse and James Bruce.

I

Captains in Conflict

The massive bows of the world's biggest troopship were scything through the heavy Atlantic swell at $28\frac{1}{2}$ knots. Six days out from New York, she was carrying 10,000 American troops, five times her peacetime passenger complement, bound for Gourock on the Clyde. The date was 2nd October 1942, and she was crossing the Atlantic at the height of the submarine war. Yet she was not in convoy. Alone and unescorted, she relied for protection on one priceless asset—her speed.

This was the giant Cunarder *Queen Mary*, 81,237 tons, 340 yards long, a target that it seemed no torpedo could miss. Yet her only concession to the submarine danger lay in her zig-zag course. Every few minutes, to a pre-set but secret schedule, she changed her heading, sometimes to port, sometimes to starboard, sometimes by 25 degrees, sometimes by 50, confusing any submarine commander who might find himself briefly within range, yet always making good her course for Britain. Because of her zig-zagging, however, her actual progress over her mean course was reduced by 2 knots.

Captain Gordon Illingworth, 'the lovable little seaman with the fog-horn voice', as he was dubbed by a contemporary, was on his first round trip as master of the *Queen Mary*. A veteran of the Battle of Jutland, he had served with Cunard or their predecessors since 1910 and was one of their senior commanders. He knew that in mid-Atlantic he had been comparatively safe. The greatest hazards of the voyage lay immediately ahead, approaching the Irish coast. Here, 150 miles off Bloody Foreland, he would come within striking distance of the German long-range aircraft preying on the Western Approaches, the Focke-Wulf Condors whose bombs were feared even more than the hazards of mine and torpedo. To counteract this threat, and to meet the increasing danger from submarines in this area, he would rendezvous at 12 degrees West with a special Royal Naval task force.

Captain John Boutwood, the sandy-haired, parchment-complexioned captain of His Majesty's cruiser *Curacoa,* and the officer in charge of the task force, was another veteran seaman. 43 years old, he had served in the Royal Navy without a break since 1917. The force he now commanded consisted of the *Curacoa* and six destroyers, his task to bring the *Queen Mary* safely into the Clyde.

There was not much that Boutwood didn't know about this kind of work. Three times in the previous two months he had escorted the *Queen Mary* through this area on outward or return Atlantic crossings, and he had done the same for the *Queen Elizabeth.* Before the *Queen Mary's* outward crossing this time he had called on her new commander to agree tactics with him.

Boutwood's main difficulty was that his ship was slower than the *Queen Mary,* even when that ship was pursuing the zig-zag course they had agreed on. The *Curacoa* had been laid down in 1916. She was one of several old cruisers that had been re-armed for anti-aircraft duties in 1939. Her top speed, with her rivets rattling, was 25 knots. Boutwood therefore laid his plans to give the maximum possible protection to the *Queen Mary* for the longest possible time. Because her best defence still lay in her speed he could not ask her to slacken off, so at some stage she would overtake him. His object therefore became to take up station ahead of her, and then, before she overtook him, to increase to maximum speed, staying as close as he could for as long as possible. By these means he would be able to offer reasonable protection until she came within the cover of shore-based fighters.

His best position in the event of air attack would be about

half a mile from the *Queen Mary,* which with so huge a ship was almost uncomfortably close. And to add to his difficulties the *Queen Mary* would still be zig-zagging, whereas he would have to maintain an absolutely steady course to keep up. The *Queen Mary,* however, as the overtaking ship, was under an obligation to keep clear of him. Article 24 of the Collision Regulations made that abundantly clear.

Boutwood had sailed with his force from Belfast on 30th September, to keep a rendezvous with the *Queen Mary* of 0700 hours on 2nd October. The weather at first was fair, but in the early hours of the morning of 2nd October the wind freshened, and it was still blowing strongly at dawn. The sea roughened and there was a heavy westerly swell. Because of damage previously sustained when steaming full out under similar conditions, all boats and other safety equipment on the *Curacoa* were lashed down.

Even more handicapped by the heavy sea was the destroyer screen, and soon after daylight the senior officer of the destroyers signalled Boutwood to say that the screen could not do more than 20 knots without risking damage. As Boutwood's orders specifically precluded him from taking such a risk, it was clear that the destroyers, when they came within range, would be rapidly overtaken.

Boutwood, however, had received a signal to say that the *Queen Mary* would be two hours late at the rendezvous, and at 07.24 he gave orders to the destroyer screen to turn back on an easterly course at eight o'clock and to sweep ahead of the *Queen Mary* at 16 knots. This would delay the point of overtaking and allow them to form a close screen in the most dangerous waters.

Another point to be decided was whether the *Curacoa* could steam safely at 25 knots when she turned round and encountered the following sea. So after detaching the destroyers Boutwood turned his ship through 180 degrees, decided that steaming at top speed would be possible, and then turned back towards the rendezvous, dropping down to 13 knots. The officers on the bridge of the *Curacoa* were now scanning the horizon for the *Queen Mary,* but so far there was no sign.

Just before nine o'clock they spotted an aircraft flying towards them. Thankfully they identified it as a Flying Fortress which had previously flown out ahead of them to spot the *Queen Mary* and which was now radioing the ship's position to them. Boutwood changed course to the north to complete his interception and soon afterwards they saw her, a grey shape on the horizon, 15 miles distant and slightly to the north.

Boutwood changed course again to line himself up ahead of her. The distance between the two ships began to close rapidly, and at 09.25 Boutwood turned through 180 degrees on to an easterly course and began to work up to full speed. The Fortress was still circling overhead. By 10 o'clock he had reached 23 knots and the *Queen Mary* was rather more than five miles behind him, almost dead astern. The interception was going according to plan and Boutwood called to his engine-room for his maximum speed of 25 knots. On her zigzag course the *Queen Mary* was now overtaking the *Curacoa* at about 1½ knots and would pass her soon after 2 o'clock.

When the two ships were near enough to signal each other by lamp the *Curacoa* asked the *Queen Mary* for her course and speed. The *Queen Mary* gave these as 108 degrees, 26 knots. Later she amended her speed to the precomputed figure of 26½ knots. It was essential that Boutwood steer the same course as the mean course of the *Queen Mary* if he was to remain in contact with her for the optimum period, and he turned on to 108 degrees. At 12.20 he signalled the *Queen Mary,* again by lamp. 'I am doing my best speed, 25 knots, on course 108 degrees. When you are ahead I will edge in astern of you.'

The officer of the watch on the bridge of the *Queen Mary* when that message was received was 34-year-old Noel Robinson, senior first officer of the ship. He had come on duty at noon, relieving the junior first officer, Stanley Wright, who had passed on to him details of the mean and zig-zag courses and the position of the cruiser. Except when Illingworth himself came out on to the bridge, the senior officer of the watch was in charge of the ship. With him on this watch Robinson had two quartermasters who would take turns to steer the ship, two look-out men—one on the bridge and one in the crow's nest—and the junior officer of the watch, Albert Hewitt. Hewitt's duties, however, were mainly navigational and he spent most of his time in the chart room.

Every few minutes the alarm bell of the zig-zag clock rang in the wheelhouse. John Lockhart, the quartermaster at the wheel, checked the next change of course, which was posted up in front of him in three columns—time, the number of degrees of the alteration, and the new course. He then rang a buzzer to warn Robinson that he was about to change course, and Robinson came to the voice-pipe and gave him permission to carry on. On this zig-zag, designated No. 8, there were nine changes of heading per hour.

With the *Curacoa* roughly dead ahead, the *Queen Mary* on these zig-zag courses was crossing and re-crossing the *Curacoa*'s wake.

At 12.30 Captain Boutwood went to his sea cabin one deck below the bridge for lunch. Just before one o'clock the Fortress, which had continued circling throughout the morning, signalled that it was leaving, and Boutwood then returned to the bridge. He noticed at once that, whereas the two ships had earlier been on about the same line of advance, the *Queen Mary* was now northwards of the cruiser, about two miles astern and some distance to port, too far, in Boutwood's estimation, for proper protection. The *Curacoa*, indeed, was clear of the *Queen Mary*'s zig-zag; the *Queen Mary* was no longer crossing and re-crossing her wake.

Now that the Fortress was gone, Boutwood was doubly anxious to keep in close. In the next two or three hours the risk of air attack would be greater than at any other time. He therefore ordered a change of course from 108 degrees to 105, and then, when this didn't bring the ships into line, to 100.

At 13.24 the *Queen Mary,* in accordance with her zig-zag, made her second turn to starboard within a few minutes, and by 13.30 she was very fine on the cruiser's port quarter, with two minutes of her starboard zig-zag still to run. It was clear to Captain Boutwood that on this leg she would cross his wake from port to starboard, which meant that he had corrected sufficiently, so he came back on to his original course of 108 degrees.

At 13.32 the zig-zag clock rang in the wheelhouse of the *Queen Mary* and Robinson gave orders for the swing on to the next leg—a 50 degree turn to port. This would take her back on to the port side of the cruiser. The distance between the two ships had narrowed considerably and was now not much more than a thousand yards. Robinson, indeed, thought it might be very much less. In a moment of un-easiness he ordered Lockhart, at the wheel, to stop the 50 degree swing to port before it was half completed and to steady up on that heading. He was afraid of running into the stern of the cruiser. He would complete the turn, he decided, when he judged it safe to do so. But at that moment Stanley Wright, the man who had done the morning watch, arrived on the bridge to relieve him for lunch.

Robinson had noticed the cruiser's small changes of course and he thought she must be operating some modified form of zig-zag to keep within protective distance. He discussed the situation with Wright. 'We're on the 50 degree port leg of the zig-zag, taking us from 131 to 081, but I've checked her at about 102. You may be able to get round all right. She's been first on one bow and then the other, and when we pass her she's going to edge in astern.' He then went below for lunch.

Wright's reaction was to try to complete the leg, and he

ordered Lockhart to swing on to 081 degrees. But before the turn was completed he decided, as Robinson had done, that the *Curacoa* was getting too close to be comfortable. He ordered Lockhart to steady the helm, then told him to starboard 5 degrees. That would give him time to think.

It seemed to him that he was bearing right down on the *Curacoa*. He didn't like it at all. His feeling was that if he continued on his present course he might run the cruiser down. His next zig-zag was to starboard, and he decided to begin it at once.

'Hard a-starboard!'

The tension in Wright's voice made it carry. Captain Illingworth, sitting in the chart room plotting the ship's position, overheard the order and came straight out on the bridge. Only some serious emergency could have stimulated such an order.

'What's the matter, Wright?'

'I don't like this cruiser, sir. She's a bit too close to me.'

'Let me have a look at her.'

Illingworth went out on to the port wing of the bridge. He judged at once that his ship could cross quite safely under the stern of the *Curacoa*. The two ships were not so close to each other as Wright and Robinson had imagined.

'No, that's all right. Put your helm amidships and come back on course. Port, and come on to 081.'

In Captain Illingworth's estimation they would clear the stern of the *Curacoa* by about half a mile. Before returning to the chart room he spoke again to Wright, his fog-horn voice reverberating for all to hear. 'Carry on with the zig-zag. These chaps are used to escorting and they won't interfere with you. They'll keep out of your way.'

In Captain Illingworth's view, his vessel was the 'stand on' ship—the one obliged to hold its course—and the cruiser the 'give-way' ship. It was his primary duty to adhere to his speed and zig-zag. It was an escort's duty to keep clear of the escorted vessel and not to add to her hazards by getting in the way. Article 21 of the Collision Regulations made that abundantly clear.

Thus the captains of the two ships, in their separate ways, both had marine law on their side. Both now settled down in the sure and certain confidence that if their two vessels got on to converging courses—as was quite likely if the *Queen Mary* pursued her zig-zag and continued crossing and re-crossing the *Curacoa*'s track—the other would give way.

Two minutes later the *Queen Mary* crossed from starboard to port of the *Curacoa*. Estimates of the distance separating the two ships varied. Some thought it was as little as a quarter of a mile. But anyway it was enough, and Illingworth's judgment was vindicated.

Many of the off-duty members of the crew of the *Curacoa* had congregated on her stern to view the Queen Mary as she went by, and they had a magnificent view of her at this time, bow-wave roaring, bows and superstructure towering above them. An officer on the upper bridge of the cruiser was busy with his camera. 'Don't miss that,' said one of his colleagues. 'It's not very often you'll get a photo of her as close as that.'

Meanwhile on every deck of the *Queen Mary* and through every port-hole, American troops were crowding round to get their first sight of the Royal Navy in action in the shape of the *Curacoa,* still an impressive sight in spite of her age as she churned up the water in the autumn sunshine.

At 13.40 the *Queen Mary* straightened up on to her mean course, slightly to port and still some way astern of the cruiser. After four minutes on the same course as the cruiser she turned away further to port on the next leg of her zig-zag and continued on that course for the next eight minutes, until 13.52. She then turned 50 degrees to starboard, back towards the cruiser.

Aboard the *Curacoa,* Captain Boutwood was taking compass bearings of the *Queen Mary* from the upper bridge. From these bearings he estimated that he was still being overtaken at $1\frac{1}{2}$ knots. But the *Queen Mary*'s precise headings in this period were difficult to compute, partly because of the time lag during her frequent turns, partly because of the considerable yaw that the cruiser was suffering in the following sea, amounting to as much as four degrees either side. To Boutwood it seemed that for much of this period the *Queen Mary* was on a roughly parallel course, having perhaps abandoned her zig-zag to overtake him. And indeed at 2 o'clock the *Queen Mary* did come back on to her mean course, parallel with the *Curacoa,* her stem almost abeam, about 1,000 yards to port.

For Boutwood, everything was going according to plan. The *Queen Mary,* at a discreet distance, was overtaking him steadily. In a few minutes, as he had indicated in his signal, he would edge in astern of her. Indeed, his mind was looking forward to other matters. At 13.55 he had signalled Illingworth: 'Please give me your estimated time of arrival at Toward Point.' This was their pinpoint on the Firth of Clyde. And Captain Illingworth was in the chart room working it out.

The 2 o'clock change on to the mean course had been made by quartermaster John Leyden, who had taken over from Lockhart at 13.59. It took about three minutes to bring the ship on to her new course. A further change of course, of 25 degrees to starboard, was due one minute later, at 14.04.

Stanley Wright, the officer of the watch on board the *Queen Mary,* was suffering from the same optical illusion that had afflicted Captain Boutwood: it seemed to him that the two ships had been on roughly parallel courses for some time. As the *Queen Mary* had been zig-zagging, he concluded that the *Curacoa* must be zig-zagging too, in order to hold her position. The fact that the *Curocoa* could not conform to the *Queen Mary*'s zig-zag without rapidly falling behind did not at first occur to him, or if it did he concluded that she must be making a better speed than she had signalled. In any case there was nothing to worry about—he had the captain's assurance that she would keep out of the way. He had been told to stick to the zig-zag, and he confirmed the 25-degree alteration to starboard when Leyden, the helmsman, spoke to him on the voice-pipe at four minutes past two.

From the upper bridge of the *Curacoa*, the view aft was somewhat obscured by the range-finder; and at that moment the masts of the destroyer screen were sighted on the horizon dead ahead, diverting attention from the Queen Mary. It was Able Seaman Norman Good, the bridge messenger, who drew Boutwood's attention to the fact that the Queen Mary was getting uncomfortably close.

Boutwood and the other officers on the upper bridge began to have doubts as to whether the liner was in fact still steering a parallel course. It was natural that they should all want to watch the ship closely as she overtook; even in her wartime grey camouflage paint she was a thrilling sight. Yet because she reacted slowly to her helm, and because the *Curacoa* was still yawing from side to side, all four officers on the bridge remained in a state of doubt.

'I think she may be turning,' said Lieutenant Johnson, the navigating officer. 'Or is it only a yaw?'

By eight minutes past two it had become clear to Boutwood and his officers that the *Queen Mary* had indeed altered to starboard. It could only be a momentary change, however, perhaps to avoid some floating object which might be a mine. If this were the case, though, the *Queen Mary* would surely sound a warning, and no such signal came.

'She's turning all right.'

Boutwood was confident that the master of the *Queen Mary* would be fully aware that the *Curacoa* must hold her course to keep up. He had never agreed to conform to any zig-zag. And one thing he knew with absolute conviction was that no ship approaching from astern would ever alter in such a manner as to endanger another ship.

At that moment Albert Hewitt, the officer who had been

on watch with Noel Robinson from noon until 13.30, returned to the *Queen Mary*'s bridge from lunch. He could just see the masts of the destroyers on the horizon, but his attention was quickly diverted to the cruiser. She seemed to be hardly more than a quarter of a mile away, on a converging course, and he guessed she must be coming in to use her loud hailer. It was the first time he had seen her on this voyage, and he walked out on to the starboard wing of the bridge to look at her through a telescope. 'I've met some of her officers,' he told Wright, 'and I'll see who's up there.' He focused on the bridge but couldn't recognise anyone, though he did see that one of the *Curacoa*'s officers was operating a camera. He put down the telescope and scanned the whole length of the ship without being conscious of any danger.

At nine minutes past two Noel Robinson came up from the dining saloon and walked through the wheelhouse to the starboard wing of the bridge. He ran into Wright just outside the wheelhouse door. 'We're going on the same course and speed,' said Wright, giving the details to Robinson. 'The captain wants me in the chart room.' And he hurried off. Captain Illingworth had sent for Wright to check his arithmetic for the arrival time at Toward Point. Thus with the two ships little more than a quarter of a mile apart and still converging, the responsibility for the safe navigation of the *Queen Mary* changed hands.

Wright did not mention the incident that had occurred during Robinson's absence, but William Heighway, the junior third and an Australian, did. 'The captain says the zig-zag legs are to be carried out in full,' he told Robinson.

'Right.'

Robinson immediately checked the *Curacoa*'s position in relation to his own. He reckoned she was about 45 degrees on his starboard bow and about 400 yards distant. He then looked at the repeater compass and checked the course of his own ship. As Wright had told him, they were steady on 131. He thought the cruiser was coming in unnecessarily close, but there was no danger in it. A touch of starboard helm and the cruiser would swing clear.

On the *Curacoa*, Captain Boutwood at this moment was not particularly alarmed either. But as a precautionary measure, and realising that he was in a situation that could quickly become dangerous, he gave an order to the helmsman.

'Starboard 15.'

This, decided Boutwood, was sufficient to keep an adequate distance between the two ships. He was still expecting the *Queen Mary* to return to her mean course at any moment.

In that following sea the cruiser did not respond to her rudder for several seconds. And her yaw at that moment, accentuated perhaps by the forces of interaction that were coming into play between the two ships because of their proximity, had risen to seven degrees to port. Eventually, however, the yaw and the invisible forces of interaction were overcome and the cruiser began to respond. Yet before the turn had been completed, Boutwood became aware that the *Queen Mary*, seeming to alter more and more to starboard, was narrowing the distance between them at an alarming rate.

To Boutwood it still seemed inconceivable that any ship in the act of overtaking would starboard into him in this way. Yet a situation that a few moments ago had seemed well under control, calling for no great concern, now seemed one of deadly danger. He moved at once to the gyro compass, thereby indicating that he was taking control of his ship.

On the bridge of the *Queen Mary*, Noel Robinson still had no real thought of collision. But he was just as puzzled as Boutwood, and he was beginning to doubt whether, if he did nothing himself, action by the other vessel, which like Boutwood he was expecting and like Boutwood believed he had every right to expect, would save the situation unaided. In spite of the order about the zig-zags he therefore gave a precautionary order to the helmsman.

'Port a little.'

Leyden, at the helm, interpreted this as an alteration of about a point—say 10 degrees. He could see nothing from the wheelhouse. He was just putting the helm over when Robinson appeared in the wheelhouse door to check that the alteration was being properly made.

While he was there Robinson consulted the zig-zag clock to see when the next routine alteration was due. The time was just after 14.10 and the next alteration was due in less than two minutes at 14.12. It was an alteration to port and would take them away from the cruiser.

Robinson hurried back to the fore part of the bridge by the voice-pipe to take another look at the cruiser. To his horror he saw that the *Curacoa* had still not altered course perceptibly and that the two ships were a mere 150 yards apart. A collision seemed imminent.

'Hard a-port!'

There was no way in which the *Queen Mary* could reduce her speed. Stopping her engines and reversing them would have no effect whatever for several minutes. Even the order to hard a-port would be governed by the same forces of inertia that delayed all her changes of heading. In the seconds available before the collision that now looked inevitable, the effect would be practically nil. Meanwhile it would be Captain Boutwood's desperate concern to avoid the unavoidable as the *Queen Mary* steamed relentlessly on.

Boutwood dare not increase his turn to starboard for fear of swinging his port quarter into the oncoming ship. Now, as the huge liner bore down on the cruiser, about a hundred feet forward of her stern, his only chance seemed to him to be to steady his helm and even to port at the last in the hope that the *Queen Mary* might miss him astern.

On the stern of the *Curacoa*, some of the men who had been watching the *Queen Mary* began to run forward in an effort to get beyond the point where the liner seemed likely to strike. Others stood transfixed in horrified disbelief.

20 miles off the Irish Coast, in bright sunshine and perfect visibility, two ships that had been in company and in regular contact by signal for many hours, with no enemy forces threatening, and with nothing else in sight except the masts of friendly destroyers, seemed about to annihilate each other.

Captain Boutwood's last-minute alteration of helm, whatever it was, came too late. Several seconds before the impact he saw the impossibility of escaping. Not until the last five seconds did the *Queen Mary* appear to steady up and begin her swing to port. Then, towering above the cruiser like a leviathan, she crashed into her at an acute angle just forward of her after-director, about two-thirds of the way down her port side.

As metal struck metal and the first jolt was felt in the two ships, the shrill, insistent ring of the zig-zag clock reverberated through the *Queen Mary*'s wheelhouse, fixing the time of the collision at precisely twelve minutes past two.

At first it seemed remotely possible that the blow might be a glancing one, that the two ships, badly mauled, staggering under the impact, might somehow recover themselves and escape mortal damage. But this hope took no account of the relative sizes of the two ships. 81,000 tons was opposed to a mere 4,500. The bows of the *Queen Mary* pushed the cruiser round to make an angle of 90 degrees, then rode straight over the top of her, and within seconds those knife-edged bows had cut right through. The two halves of the *Curacoa*, writhing like some severed worm, were separated by the vast bulk of the *Queen Mary* as she bull-dozed inexorably on.

Whatever the effect might be on the *Queen Mary*, the *Curacoa* was surely doomed. The forepart lay on her beam ends, the stern turned turtle, baring her screws to the sky. Clouds of smoke enveloped both sections and the hiss of escaping steam was deafening. When the *Queen Mary* finally passed through the gap, the two sections were separated by over a hundred yards.

Of the *Curacoa*'s complement of 430 men, some were already dead, others were dying, others were drowning, many were trapped. But the vast majority of them were clinging tenaciously but precariously to life. What hope was there for them? The wreckage of the ship would sink within minutes. Boats might be impossible to launch. The destroyers were almost out of sight on the horizon. That, for any hope of immediate rescue—before exposure in the icy seas began to claim its victims—left only the *Queen Mary* herself.

The giant Cunarder that had wrought their destruction now loomed as a bulwark of hope. But the *Queen Mary* too had suffered damage. And every minute she lingered in these waters would endanger the lives of her 10,000 American troops.

The conversation in the chart room of the *Queen Mary* seconds before the collision had been of mundane things. Stanley Wright, the junior first officer, had just finished checking Captain Illingworth's figures for his arrival time at Toward Point on the Clyde. The *Queen Mary* was due to arrive there in little more than four hours' time, at 18.30 hours, 2nd October.

'I think that's about as accurate as we can get it, sir,' said Wright.

'I think so too,' said Illingworth. 'Send for the signalman and make the signal.'

At that moment the two men felt a bump. Illingworth thought they might have been hit by a bomb from an enemy plane, and he hurried out on to the bridge, followed by Wright. As they passed the wheelhouse Illingworth spoke to the helmsman.

'Was that a bomb?'

'No sir, we hit the cruiser.'

American troops at various vantage points had watched in mute amazement as the two ships pursued their converging courses. But because of the liner's great length and height few of them actually witnessed the collision. Now, as they rushed to fresh vantage points, some of them saw that the *Curacoa* had been cut in half. The stern was floating by to starboard, end up in the water with the propellers still turning, partly obscured by thick yellow smoke. Then on the port side they saw the cruiser's bow, listing drunkenly and also enveloped in smoke and steam.

What damage had the *Queen Mary* suffered? What shape was she in to carry out a rescue operation? Would she be able to make port herself?

Harry Grattridge, staff captain of the *Queen Mary*, was asleep on his bunk in his sea cabin when he felt the jolt. He crammed on his tin hat, flung on his duffle-coat, and ran to the bridge. 'Look, sir!' shouted Robinson. The two broken sections of the *Curacoa* lay dead astern. But he noticed that the *Mary* was still steaming at full speed. Everyone was looking towards Captain Illingworth for the signal to turn back.

A quick inspection of the *Queen Mary*'s forepeak had already been made. 'The stem's pushed back and the forepeak's awash,' reported the bos'n. Illingworth gave orders to reduce speed while Grattridge hurried through the alleyway down to the forepeak to make a more thorough inspection. Water was racing in and out of the forepeak; if it penetrated the collision bulkhead, the watertight steel wall that sprouted from the base of the ship to the main deck, the *Queen Mary* might not survive. But there was not a crack, not a fissure. The bulkhead had held. 'I was sick,' wrote Harry Grattridge afterwards, 'at what we had done, yet I marvelled, too, at the strange and terrible impregnability of the *Queen Mary*. It came home to me that she had no equal anywhere in the Atlantic, perhaps not anywhere in the world.'

After giving orders to strengthen the bulkhead, Grattridge went back to the bridge and reported to Captain Illingworth. It seemed that the *Queen Mary* could safely turn back. At this moment the aft section of the dismembered cruiser, screws still uppermost, sank beneath the swell, leaving a pall of smoke that dispersed slowly, revealing only a handful of survivors from this section.

Captain Illingworth was facing an appalling choice. The *Queen Mary*'s principal defence in these dangerous waters lay in her speed, coupled with her frequent changes of course. Either he turned back to pick up survivors, deliberately hazarding his ship with its many thousands of passengers, or he steamed on, leaving hundreds of men to their fate.

If he signalled the destroyers, which were almost out of sight on the horizon, it would be several hours before they could reach the area against the heavy sea. By that time, scores of men would almost certainly have succumbed from exposure and shock.

Although Illingworth had not yet had time to appraise the collision in detail, he was confident that the cruiser must herself be to blame. Yet considerations of who was at fault were dwarfed for the moment by the terrible dilemma in which he was placed. All his instincts of humanity and comradeship urged him to turn back and pick up the men whose task it had been to protect him. All his experience as a seaman and master warned him to sail on.

Even as he recoiled from his decision, Captain Illingworth recognised the inevitability of it. Seamanship must come first, humanity second. The safety of his 10,000 passengers, and of his ship, must be his only consideration.

'Tell those destroyers what's happened,' he ordered. 'Ask them to move in and pick up survivors.'

Captain Illingworth had virtually passed sentence of death on scores of men who might otherwise have survived.

The wake of the *Queen Mary* did not deviate; she sailed straight on for the Clyde.

The majority of the men of the *Curacoa* were still involved in a desperate struggle for survival. To those for whom the *Queen Mary* was still visible, it seemed that the liner was steaming on. But they remembered her huge turning circle, and how long it took her to change course. She would be back to pick them up as soon as she could. With this thought to sustain them they redoubled their efforts to get clear.

When the collision came Captain Boutwood hung on to the rail of the upper bridge as the ship heeled over. The other officers on the bridge did the same.

21-year-old Bob Markham, one of the many Hull reservists on board, ran forward along the gun deck from 'B' gun amidships, just abaft the funnels, when he realised that the *Queen Mary* wasn't going to turn away. Several other members of the gun crew ran with him. One man tripped and fell in the rush to get clear. He was not seen again.

Markham had reached the break of the forecastle when the collision came. He was just in time to cling like a monkey to the port side guard rail as the ship went over. Below him the deck dropped sheer as a wall.

Stan Farrow, another Hull reservist on 'B' gun, stayed where he was, grabbing the gun-shield to steady himself. But the impact wrenched him from his grip and threw him on to the second of the two funnels, burning him severely. He struggled to get clear but was pinned by the force of gravity as the ship lay on her side.

Bob Gornall, 37 and a long-service seaman, had been born with a caul. That, according to superstition, meant that he couldn't drown. At the time of the collision he was asleep in the mess-deck just underneath the bridge. He rushed out on to the aft part of the bridge to see what had happened, but by this time the fore part of the ship had taken an alarming angle and he was obliged to hold on.

Stoker Harry Ellis, another Hull man, had come up, like many others during their off-duty period, to watch the liner overtake them. As the *Curacoa* didn't seem to be taking any evasive action Ellis began to run forward. When he reached the companion way leading up to the forecastle head he looked back. The stem of the *Queen Mary* towered above him, completely obliterating the sky. He could not even see her superstructure. Then she struck, just about where he had been standing half a minute earlier.

Ellis had his hand firmly on the rail of the companionway, but as the ship heeled over he lost his grip and was thrown into the water. He went under, and then something brushed against his finger-tips and he grabbed at it—it was the starboard rail, several feet under water. In that swirling vortex of foam it offered support, and although obliged to hold his breath he retained his grip, his lungs bursting. Presently, as he had hoped, the ship began to right itself and he broke to the surface and breathed gloriously. Then he began to scramble up the sloping deck. Eventually he regained the ladder from which he had been thrown.

Below decks the men thought they had been torpedoed. Harry Bell, strong and volatile, first man in of the Hull volunteers, was one of the eight-man crew of the H.A.C.P. (High Angle Control Position), the team that plotted the radar and visual sightings and fed the predictions to the guns. He was also a great friend of Bob Markham, to whom his wife's sister was engaged.

As the ship went over, water poured down the ventilator shaft into the restricted area of the H.A.C.P., with its central plotting table and low head-room. The men managed to escape through a wash-room, but eight or nine watertight doors separated them from the nearest exit to the deck. Their best hope lay in the engine-room uptake—the air uptake that carried the fumes away from the engine-room. There was no ladder in this uptake, but the list of the ship might make scrambling up possible.

As they clambered up they realised that the gratings at the top were still fixed firmly in place. There was no way of removing them from underneath. But the Engineer-Commander, Douglas Robertson, foreseeing that some of his engine-room staff might attempt to escape this way, had removed the gratings by the time they reached the top. Somehow the entire crew of the H.A.C.P. got out through the grating and on to the gun deck.

Engineer-Commander Robertson was by this time attending to a badly injured man. He was making no attempt to leave the ship himself.

Edgar ('Tug') Wilson, another Hull reservist, had gone off watch at 12.30, had lunch, and then had a bath prior to catching up with his washing. The bathroom he was using was forward, and he was sitting on a stool in vest and underpants and heavy sea-boots, rinsing out his washing in a bucket. He had no lifejacket with him. The next moment there was a paralysing jerk, the stool shot from under him, the bucket crashed into a corner, and all the lights went out. Wilson managed to crawl outside into the passage and scramble up to the deck. He was still in his underwear, and he still had no lifejacket. When he got up on to the forecastle head he made for the boats.

All the boats on the starboard side had been crushed like matchwood, but Wilson climbed into the port whaler, where he found a supply of lifejackets. A petty officer named Downey was trying to launch the whaler, but the list to starboard was jamming the boat on its davits and they couldn't push it out.

Marine Eric Bower, a regular, just 21, was asleep on a mess-deck stool slightly aft of amidships, not far forward of the point of impact. When the collision came he was thrown across the mess-deck from one side to the other, a distance of about 30 feet. The lights went out, and as the ship went over everyone in the mess-deck was thrown on top of him and he finished up in a tangle of arms and legs and bodies on the starboard side in complete darkness. To intensify the horror of it, a length of loose cable had been thrown into the same corner and was becoming intertwined with the men. Bower thought he would be either strangled or suffocated.

There was a ladder leading to the upper deck, with a hatch at the top that was kept closed, locked by three cleats. Men were scrambling up the ladder as a column of water flooded the mess-deck. Bower, blue-eyed and crinkly-haired but strong and wiry too, fought his way clear of the cable and the heap of bodies to the foot of the ladder, where he was up to his waist in water. Men behind him were shoving violently and shouting at those above them to hurry.

At last they got the hatch undone, and one by one they clambered out on to the main deck. It too was awash. Waves were breaking into and over the jagged structure amidships where the *Queen Mary* had carved her way through. Above them a broken mast, smashed as the ship bent over, was swinging and banging against the superstructure.

As Bower emerged from the hatch a huge wave broke over him and he was nearly washed overboard. He had no life-belt, and he decided to climb up to the comparative safety of the gun deck. As the ship was still listing at 45 degrees, scrambling up the superstructure looked feasible. Several other men climbed up with him.

Ronnie Heavens, the captain's steward, was in the aft part of the ship, having just helped to serve the officers' lunch. The *Queen Mary* cut through within a few feet of where he stood, and as the mess-deck collapsed around him he dropped straight into the water. By a miracle he struggled clear.

One of the stokers who was down in the stoke-hold stepped into the sea as the *Queen Mary* sliced through. Completely naked, he was quickly covered in a film of oil. He struck out at once to get clear of the turbulent whirlpool of water that surrounded the wreckage.

Another man still alive from the aft section was seaman Ernest Watson, a Devonian. He had been watching the *Queen Mary* and had realised the danger too late. As the stern turned turtle he was flung into the water. Fortunately he was wearing a lifebelt.

Although the aft section had foundered so rapidly, the fore part of the vessel seemed at first to right itself, and Boutwood began to think there might be a chance of saving it. But he quickly realised this was a forlorn hope. With the great volume of water that was pouring into her from the gaping hole aft of her funnels she must sink within minutes. 'Go down and take charge of what ratings you can find,' he shouted to his officers. 'Get the life-saving equipment ready for use.' But all efforts to launch the boats were unsuccessful because of the heavy list. Even many of the buoyant flotta nets, lashed down because of the weather, were impossible to release. Several such nets, however, were somehow torn free and pushed overboard.

Below him Boutwood could hear his officers transmitting his orders to abandon ship. He himself elected to remain on the bridge. Then the ship began to heel over to starboard again, and as he held on to the bridge he watched scores of his men sliding across the sloping deck or struggling to gain the port hand-rail and haul themselves through.

When they had time to pause for a moment in their frenzied efforts to save themselves, the men of the *Curacoa* turned their gaze fleetingly towards the *Queen Mary*. Stunned by what they saw, they watched in mute despair as her stern receded.

When he heard the order to abandon ship Tug Wilson hurried back to the forecastle head. He had reached the guard rail when the ship went over for the second time, and he was able to crawl through and sit for a moment on the ship's side, which was now horizontal. Then he slid down her plates into the water, carefully avoiding the rolling chocks above the keel as he went. Once in the water he kicked off his sea-boots and started swimming to get clear of the ship, which seemed about to capsize.

Bob Gornall slid over the side at about the same time and found himself perched on the rolling chocks. Then a wave broke over him and he lost his grip and was launched into the sea. The coldness of it, even on this bland autumn day, struck him like a blow.

The *Curacoa,* lying horizontal on her starboard side, was providing a precarious launching platform for those of her crew who had been quick or lucky enough to gain the port side and climb through the rail. As though flung unexpectedly on to some unpredictable moving staircase, men in all stages of dress and undress, some in rubber boots and some barefoot, some with lifejackets and some without, were fighting to keep their balance on the slippery plates as the ship heaved like some sea monster in agony. One by one, in a confused and kaleidoscopic pattern, they pursued their erratic way down the ship's side. Many lost their balance and slid rapidly towards the sea. Some struck the steel rim of the rolling chocks and somersaulted into the water, injuring themselves severely. Others fell clear into the sea.

Harry Ellis, with two others, was trying to release a cork flotta net just under the bridge when the ship heeled over for the second time. He managed to reach the port rail, then ran down the side and jumped.

The men who escaped from the H.A.C.P., Harry Bell among them, were just in time to grab the port rail and swarm over the side; they too stared in helpless astonishment as the *Queen Mary* disappeared in the distance. Bob Markham and Stan Farrow, from 'B' gun, had become separated, but each walked calmly down the ship's side and dived in.

Eric Bower jumped from the upper deck back to the main deck, determined to keep on top of the ship as she rolled. Many of the men he was with went in the other direction, sliding down towards the starboard side, but he thought they might be trapped if the ship capsized. Everything was wet because it had either been under water or flooded by the bow-wave of the *Queen Mary,* and as he clutched at the guard rail he slipped. Somehow he hung on, but he badly twisted his ankle. Men were still trying to cut liferafts and Carley floats adrift, and Bower, still without a lifejacket, decided to make for one of these rafts when he reached the sea.

As he climbed through the rail he was one of the last to see Douglas Robertson, the engineer-commander, making his way along the upper deck, immaculately dressed in tunic, cap and gloves, waist deep in water, careless of his own safety, still intent on saving as many as possible of his men.

As soon as Bower hit the water it was as though some giant hand grabbed him and dragged him under, turning him over and over in the turbulent seas. He lost all sense of orientation and had no idea how deep he had been thrown or whether he would ever come to the surface. Then at last, fighting for breath, he broke clear. Someone was in the water alongside him but it could have been his nearest mess-mate and he wouldn't have known him—everyone was covered with oil and the faces he saw were black and shiny and unrecognisable.

The man near him, also without a lifebelt, began to clutch at him. If he catches hold of me, thought Bower, I'm finished. He barely had the strength to fight the seas himself, let alone help anyone else. Hastily and without compunction he turned his back on the man and swam as hard as he could away from him.

All the men who had got away from the *Curacoa* were trying to put as much distance as they could between the ship and themselves before she went down. All had heard stories of suction and rumours that when a ship went down her boilers burst. Such fears were exaggerated out of all proportion but they provided a spur to the men as they fought to get clear.

Stan Farrow saw a line of men clinging to the lower

boom—a horizontal mast that had broken away as the ship heeled over. As they fought and jostled for a hold it rotated like a greasy pole, throwing them off. Many of the men, exhausted by their efforts, were forced under.

Looking round to see what progress he was making, Bob Markham watched the ship slowly come up level again. Was she going to float after all? Then her bows went up in the air and she began to go down stern first. She had floated for $4\frac{1}{2}$ minutes.

Scores of men watched in awe as the bows rose almost vertically. High up in the bows, clinging to the paravanes, was a man without a lifebelt. Some claimed to recognise him as a known non-swimmer. As the bows rose he rose with them, until he was perhaps 120 feet up. Then the stern started sinking, and as the ship slid backwards in majestic slow-motion, still perpendicular, the man clinging to the paravanes waved. It was the last visible gesture of courage and comradeship to come from the *Curacoa*.

Only when they were lifted up to the top of the swell could the men in the water see the retreating stern of the *Queen Mary*. Of the destroyers there was as yet no sign. The ship which had been their home and which held all their possessions had gone to the bottom, and it seemed that they were being left to their fate. Only the strongest and toughest, both mentally and physically, were likely to survive for long.

Bob Gornall decided not to go near any of the flotta nets; his instinct warned him to keep away. Only very occasionally, when he came to the top of a wave, did he see anyone else, but he could hear voices crying out for help, many of them hysterical, as though in the last extremity. Their cries went unanswered, but there was no callousness in it; no one could help them. Their strength sapped by shock, their limbs enfeebled by cramp and their muscles weakened by cold, the survivors trusted themselves to themselves and fought to stay afloat.

For ten minutes or so after the sinking these agonised cries went on. Then, as the survivors became scattered over a wider area, men became completely isolated from each other and the cries of the drowning ceased or were no longer heard. Less than a third of the complement of the *Curacoa*, totalling 430 men, had survived this far. All the time the numbers were dwindling.

Bob Markham had a mortal dread of becoming entangled in the flotta nets, but he clung to the side of one just the same. The naked, oil-covered stoker was next to him. As more and more men piled on to the net it sank below the surface but it still remained buoyant.

Stan Farrow saw three flotta nets in all, each supporting 15 to 20 men. An officer clinging to the same net as Farrow swam off to help someone in difficulties. Farrow never saw him again.

Harry Ellis was carried well clear of the ship before it went down, but as time passed the buoyancy of his lifebelt seemed to decrease. Like many others he had taken in a lot of oil, and he knew his resistance was impaired. Eventually he passed out.

Tug Wilson was one of the few men able to give assistance to a comrade. He was swimming away from the ship when another of the Hull reservists, Jack Swabey, asked if he could hang on to him for a breather. Swabey had no lifebelt and had exhausted himself in swimming away from the ship. Both men eventually reached the flotta nets.

Eric Bower, deep in the trough of the swell for most of the time, could see nothing but sea and sky. He still had no lifebelt, and he was not a strong swimmer. If anyone had told him he could keep afloat in mid-Atlantic for three-quarters of an hour he would have scoffed—but that is what he proceeded to do. He simply kept treading water, and eventually he found himself near one of the flotta nets.

Meanwhile two of the destroyers, *Bramham* and *Cowdray*, had been detached by the senior officer of the flotilla to pick up survivors. They reached the area soon after four o'clock—nearly two hours after the collision. Then they began their search. Many of the men they picked up were already dead. Others, like Harry Ellis, were alive but unconscious. Some, like Harry Bell, had withstood the experience so well that they were able to assist, on board the destroyers, in hauling people up the scrambling nets and even diving back in to fish them out.

One of the *Bramham*'s boats became waterlogged. An exhausted survivor lay in the bottom unconscious. As the boat drew alongside the destroyer it sank. All efforts to retrieve the unconscious man failed.

Harry Bell and Bob Markham had seen nothing of each other since the collision. Both were preparing themselves for breaking the tidings to the girls on their return when they recognised each other on board the *Bramham*.

Next day the survivors were landed at Londonderry. There were 101 in all—two officers and 99 ratings—so 329 men were lost. One of the officers picked up alive was John Boutwood.

The survivors were ordered to say nothing of the incident—and they kept their word so well that the sinking of the *Curacoa* became one of the best-kept secrets of the war. The American Service authorities imposed their own security clamp-down, but in any case few of the *Queen Mary*'s passengers realised the extent of the disaster. The impact felt below decks in the liner was slight, and the severed halves of the cruiser were quickly left behind.

It was not until 1945 that the loss was revealed. Then, on 2nd March 1945, the Admiralty initiated action against Cunard for damages, claiming that the collision was caused solely by the negligent navigation of the *Queen Mary*. The Admiralty had already held their own court of enquiry into the loss of the cruiser, and since they brought the action, and

c

since Captain Boutwood received no reprimand and suffered no loss of seniority, it is clear that this enquiry must have exonerated him and his crew. But the defence put up by Cunard was spirited.

The scene in that square drab court-room off the Strand, with its Victorian Gothic arches and grim oak panelling, its musty rows of law books and high canopied dais, seemed contrived and theatrical after the harsh realities of the Atlantic war. How could the frantic last few seconds before the collision, and the decisions taken in those unforgiving moments, ever be satisfactorily reconstructed and analysed in such an austere atmosphere? Yet the battle that was fought in that court-room was scarcely less bitter than the wartime one, the collision of legal opinion almost as dramatic. The antagonists were impelled by the same deadly purpose—to seek out each other's weakness, and to destroy.

The public gallery, packed with the widows and next of kin of the men who died, had far more than a morbid interest in the proceedings. If the Admiralty won their case, the relatives could sue Cunard for damages.

As the case dragged on over many months it fluctuated first this way, then that. Cunard were able to call on six men from the bridge of the *Queen Mary*, in addition to Captain Illingworth. The Admiralty called on Captain Boutwood alone, the sole officer survivor from the bridge of the *Curacoa*. There was a second survivor, Norman Good, but although he had been a witness at the internal Admiralty court of enquiry he was not called at the court case. As he was the man who was sent to fetch the officers' cameras, and as he has since claimed that the view aft was obscured by the range-finder, that the officers on the bridge were diverted at a critical moment by their first glimpse of the destroyer screen, and that he himself drew the captain's attention to the fact that the *Queen Mary* was getting 'dangerously close', the inference that his evidence might have damaged the Admiralty's case is hard to resist.

Eventually, on 21st January 1947, Mr. Justice Pilcher delivered his judgment. He found the *Curacoa* entirely to blame.

The basis of his judgment was that the normal maritime rule for overtaking—that the overtaking ship should keep clear of the other vessel—did not apply in the situation of escort and convoy, and that the *Curacoa* was under a primary duty to keep out of the way of the *Queen Mary*. He also held that correct helm action by the cruiser could have averted the collision almost up to the last few seconds.

The judgment was a complete vindication of Captain Illingworth's view of the respective duties of the two ships as freely expressed by him little more than half an hour before the disaster. But this was by no means the end of the matter. The Admiralty appealed against the judgment, and the Court of Appeal varied it by a majority, finding both vessels clearly at fault—the *Curacoa* by two-thirds and the *Queen Mary* by one-third—and the House of Lords, to whom both parties then appealed, confirmed this judgment.

In retrospect, many may feel that an equal division of the blame might have been fairer. Indeed, this was hinted at under appeal, but not pursued. Since the question of who should give way had not been specifically agreed between the two captains beforehand, and since no instruction of any kind had been laid down on this point in the convoy orders, surely neither should have persisted in any course which might endanger the other.

It might even be held that the blame lay less with the two captains than with the authority which issued the convoy orders—presumably, in the last instance, the Admiralty. If orders are misunderstood or misinterpreted it is often the fault not so much of those who carry them out as of those who issue them, for not making them clear beyond all ambiguity or doubt.

Captain Boutwood completed a distinguished naval career in 1951. He was awarded the D.S.O. in 1943, and in

1944 he was mentioned in despatches for 'outstanding courage, resolution, leadership, skill and devotion to duty' following the landings on the Italian mainland. He told all he knew about the loss of his ship in court, and he never discussed it afterwards.

Captain Illingworth, too, had in other respects an unchequered career, marked at its peak by a knighthood. But he never forgot the *Curacoa*. 'I did everything I could to console him,' said his staff captain, Harry Grattridge. 'But often afterwards I would see him sitting at his desk in the cabin, staring into space.'

Curiously enough Captain Illingworth was never questioned in the witness box about his decision not to stop, yet Captain Boutwood was. It was the nearest the enquiry got to a direct confrontation between the two captains, and Captain Illingworth, for all his confidence in his own judgment, must have hung on to Boutwood's words. So indeed did the entire court.

'What did the *Queen Mary* do after the collision?' asked Mr. K. S. Carpmael, K.C., counsel for the Admiralty.

'She steamed on.'

'Was that the proper thing for her to do?'

Captain Boutwood's answer was little more than a whisper, but it reverberated round the silent court.

'I would say "Yes".'

On this point, at least, the two captains were agreed.

* * *

I am indebted to the recorded proceedings of the case which the Admiralty brought against Cunard in 1946—kindly lent to me by Cunard—for operational details, and I am especially grateful to those survivors of the *Curacoa* whom I was able to find for their description of the collision and of how the cruiser went down.

2

Alison Mitchell

'It's the *Mariecelia*! What's happened to her?'

The first man to see her, Stanley le Cornu, was driving along the coast road to St. Aubin on his way home from work. What was such a vessel doing out in such a sea? He carried on past St. Aubin towards Noirmont Point to get a closer look.

Passing him a moment later from the direction of Noirmont Point was another Jersey resident, William Morvan. Morvan was on his way to St. Helier to raise the alarm.

All day the port of St. Helier had been stormbound in one of the fiercest and most destructive hurricanes ever to hit the island. The date was 9th October 1964. Now here was this lone vessel, partially capsized yet apparently still under power, battling its way into the bay in the late afternoon through gale-force winds and mountainous seas.

More than a thousand telephone lines in the island had been blown down during the day, and Stanley le Cornu had to drive on past Noirmont Point to Portelet before he could find a serviceable phone. Meanwhile William Morvan had reached the South Pier Shipyard and raised the alarm.

Captain R. S. Taylor, deputy harbourmaster, got a crew together and put out at once in the pilot cutter, sending a message to the lifeboat crew to join him in the bay. He passed the pierheads at 6.5 p.m. Despite a rough, confused sea and poor visibility, Captain Taylor picked out the stricken vessel and steered towards her. As he approached he saw that her deck had been swept clean. Masts, spars, wheelhouse, deckhouse, guard-rails—all were gone. Yet the engines were running.

He was close enough now to identify her for certain. It

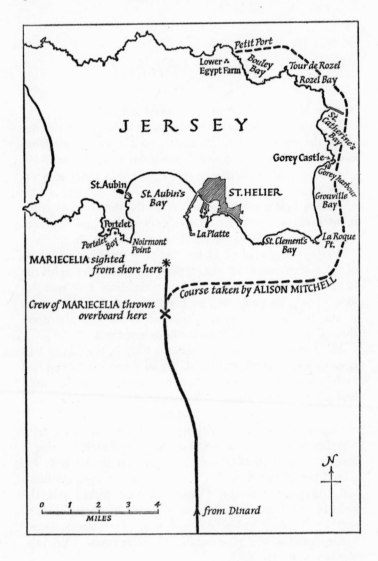

JERSEY

Petit Port
Lower Egypt Farm
Bouley Bay
Tour de Rozel
Rozel Bay
St. Catherine's Bay
Gorey Castle
Gorey harbour
St. Aubin
St. Aubin's Bay
ST. HELIER
Grouville Bay
Portelet
Portelet Bay
Noirmont Point
La Platte
St. Clement's Bay
La Roque Pt.
MARIECELIA sighted from shore here
Course taken by ALISON MITCHELL
Crew of MARIECELIA thrown overboard here

0 1 2 3 4
MILES

N

from Dinard

was the *Mariecelia* all right. A 53-foot motor yacht, registered in Jersey, she was well known in St. Helier. Captain Taylor and his crew scanned her closely, but it was clear there was no one on board. Joined by the lifeboat, he began to search further south for survivors.

Soon afterwards the *Mariecelia* foundered on the rocks to the east of the breakwater. Cutter and lifeboat went on searching until long after nightfall, but the seas became too dangerous for them. As the storm continued and visibility deteriorated they were forced to return to harbour.

Seven days earlier, on Saturday 3rd October, the *Mariecelia* had left Jersey for St. Malo on a week's cruise. On board had been a party of five. 58-year-old Jimmy Fraser, a farmer, and his wife Dolly, 53, had lived in Jersey for 15 years. Their son Robert, 25, was a Cambridge rowing blue. Mike McCowen, 26, the fourth member of the party, was an expert dinghy sailor. Completing the party was Alison Mitchell, just 21, dark and attractive, but plump and homely in figure. Accustomed to the good things in life, she knew she was overweight. One day she would do something about it.

The headlines that were set up in Fleet Street that evening inevitably concentrated on the *Mariecelia*. '106 m.p.h. Channel Wind Strikes Yacht' was one such headline. 'Five Drowned in Hurricane' was another. But somewhere out in that spumy, tempestuous void, 21-year-old Alison Mitchell was still fighting for her life.

Alison's 21st birthday had been almost exactly a month earlier, on 7th September. The party to celebrate it, given by her father at their home at Michen Hall, Shackleford, near Godalming, was still a vivid memory. It had been at that party that Robert Fraser had told her about the cruise.

'Sounds great.'

'Would you like to come?'

Would she! Her birthday present from her father had been an E-type Jaguar, and she planned a driving holiday on the Continent. She would fly back from France to Jersey to take in the cruise, then resume her tour.

For Alison the Frasers were old friends, as was Mike McCowen. He and Robert had been at Radley together, and she had known them since she was a child. The Frasers were 'courtesy' uncles and aunts—Uncle Jimmy and Auntie Dolly. She had joined them at their home at Le Maison Maret, Trinity, on 2nd October and helped them pack for the cruise. The continuing fine weather had encouraged many yacht owners to prolong the sailing season before laying up for the winter, and the weather was still perfect when they left for St. Malo next morning. The crossing was uneventful, and they spent three pleasant days cruising off the French coast.

When the weather broke on 7th October the Frasers sought the shelter of the Rance estuary at Dinard and spent the next two days exploring up-river. On Thursday it was so cold that they kindled a fire in the galley and huddled round it. That night, the last night of their holiday, they treated themselves to a farewell meal at a riverside restaurant.

When they got back to the boat at eleven o'clock to pre-pare for an early start smoke was pouring from the galley. Robert dashed ahead and grabbed a fire extinguisher, and between them they pulled the wood out of the fire. But the galley was completely burnt out, gas from the cylinders had escaped, and they were left without heat or light. For-tunately the galley was forward of the cabin and neither the two Gardner diesels nor the steering were affected by the fire.

The accident, the discomfort it caused, and concern over insurance, determined them to get back to Jersey as soon as possible. But gusts up to 65 knots had been recorded that day off the island, and unsettled weather was expected to con-tinue. It would depend on the forecast next morning.

The three men were up early to pick up the B.B.C. broad-cast at 06.40. Winds for Dover, Wight and Portland were given as westerly Force 4, gradually freshening and veering to become west to north-west Force 5 or 6, perhaps 7 in Portland later. Showers might be prolonged at times, with local thunder, but visibility would otherwise be good.

Winds of Force 5 to 6 meant up to about 30 knots, and the sea would be rough, but this need not deter them. Nevertheless the general situation promised an unpleasant crossing, and after starting up and heading down-river Jimmy Fraser went down to the cabin to talk to the women.

'Do you girls feel like flying home or can you take a rough crossing?'

Both Alison and her aunt were experienced sailors, and they had every confidence in the men. They could easily have opted to fly back, but they decided against it. For the moment they would stay in their bunks. However rough the crossing, the distance was under 40 miles, and even with a north-westerly wind it would hardly take them more than four or five hours.

They passed through the lock gates beyond Dinard at eight o'clock and set their northerly course for St. Helier. The shark—the plywood speedboat they used for water-skiing—and the dinghy were hauled on board.

There was nothing exceptional about the weather at first. It was rough, but no more so than on an averagely bad Channel crossing. After about an hour and a half, however, it got decidedly rougher, and both the women were thrown repeatedly out of their bunks. Dolly Fraser went up to the deckhouse, where her husband was studying his charts. 'This is getting a bit much,' she said.

'We're almost half-way,' said Jimmy Fraser. 'Shall we go on?'

Alison had joined them by this time and they all agreed there was no point in turning back. Had they known the latest weather news at Jersey, however, they might have changed their minds. A dramatic fall in barometric pressure to one of the lowest readings ever recorded on the island had been followed by winds of hurricane force. Trees were being uprooted, walls blown down and roof tiles lifted, dock-yard cranes swept along the front and ships in harbour wrecked. There was little chance, according to the latest forecast, of the winds diminishing before dawn next day.

At 10.15 the B.B.C. broadcast a gale warning, but it was not heard on the *Mariecelia*. All other shipping in the area sought shelter, but the *Mariecelia,* shuddering to her roots with each fresh sea, was still heading into wind, speed dras-tically reduced but still making for Jersey.

Robert and Mike put some steadying sails up, but they were ripped away at once. Alison went down to the burnt-out galley to make some sandwiches as a morale-builder for the men, but the milk in the fridge had spilled over every-thing and gone sour. Fighting back sea-sickness, she found some uncontaminated food and took the sandwiches up to the wheelhouse.

It was impossible to keep her feet in the deckhouse, and she sat on the third step down into the cabin, bracing herself in the narrow shaft. The seas were a heaving cauldron, with great scroll-topped waves breaking over the deckhouse with sledgehammer force. Dolly Fraser, sitting in the deckhouse, was thrown so heavily to the floor that she badly injured her arm.

Alison realised the arm was broken, but lacking a steady platform to work from there was little she could do. She helped her aunt wedge herself as best she could where she was.

Half an hour later a great piledriver of a wave struck the forward window of the deckhouse with terrific impact, shat-tering the glass and bursting into the saloon, showering it with water and scattering a barrage of broken glass. Alison and her aunt were both severely cut about the head, and the charts on which Jimmy Fraser was working were stained with brine and blood.

'We'll have to plug that hole.'

Every other sea flung itself through the aperture, flooding the saloon and pouring down the steps into the cabin. Alison went down to the bunks, grabbed a couple of mattresses and lugged them up the steps. Then she stuffed them into the hole. She cut her hands as she did so, but the mattresses held.

It was now about midday, and Robert, in the wheelhouse, had reduced speed until they were scarcely moving. But they knew they must be getting close to Jersey. Putting a harness on for safety, Mike left the wheelhouse and went forward to look for land.

From the saloon it was impossible to see anything but the surging mountain peaks of the sea, and the wheelhouse was taking such a battering that visibility up there was almost nil. Suddenly they heard Mike shouting above the storm.

'I can see land!'

They couldn't be more than three or four miles off the Jersey coast. But for half an hour after Mike's excursion forward they saw nothing, their view obscured by the giant undulations of the sea. Yet their spirits had been sustained by that fleeting glimpse of land. 'Won't it be wonderful to get home for a nice cup of hot chocolate,' said Alison. 'Yes,' said Jimmy Fraser, 'and one of Auntie Dolly's famous steak and kidney puddings.'

The time came when they could see land every third or fourth wave, and even see it sometimes from the saloon. Yet the seas were getting even more vicious. Would they be able to avoid the rocks off St. Aubin's Bay?

'Let's send an S.O.S.' Jimmy Fraser tried his voice radio, but the equipment was dead. The aerials had long since been carried away.

Suddenly they were caught up in a swirling vortex of wind and sea. It became impossible to keep the vessel headed into wind.

'Look out!'

The shout came from the wheelhouse, and a moment later

a huge blockbuster of a sea broke with seismic violence over the *Mariecelia*. With a thunderous detonation the entire superstructure, wheelhouse and deckhouse together, was swept away.

Crouching on the steps below the saloon, Alison heard the wrenching of timbers and the deafening crash of the sea, then felt herself being dragged down the steps. A sudden, impenetrable darkness was accompanied by a terrifying feeling of suffocation. She had been pitched headlong into a world containing neither light nor air.

The great column of water that had bulldozed straight through the superstructure and carried Alison to the depths of the vessel now ricocheted in an undertow of inexorable force. The suction dragged her from the cabin and flushed her towards the surface in one great cleansing gush. The darkness lifted marginally and she was conscious of light.

Stupefied, choked, paralysed, she came to the surface briefly only to sink immediately. The dark shutter that had descended before her eyes had lifted only to fall across her mind.

'Come on, old girl, you're all right.'

The voice came to her down a long corridor, incredibly distant. Yet it was right beside her. Robert had grabbed her by the hair. She could feel nothing, recall nothing, yet she gasped involuntarily for air. Robert was beside her, holding her up, and she felt enormously encouraged by his presence.

Around them floated boxes, spars, furniture, cushions, clothing—all the flotsam of shipwreck. Fifty yards away the *Mariecelia*, stripped to her decks, steamed on.

There was no hope of reboarding her. Even if they could have reached her, she stood too far out of the water. But if she held her present course she would be seen. Then someone would come and look for them.

Alison was astonished to find that they were all in the water together. Auntie Dolly's arm was painful, and Uncle

Jimmy had been injured in the face when he was swept overboard, but as they huddled together there were no recriminations. No one said isn't this awful, no one asked why this should have happened to them. They had not been wearing lifejackets, and they swam to a large wooden beam used to support the boat against quaysides and held on.

Jimmy Fraser put the time of their immersion at about 1.30. They couldn't see land from the water, but the tide must still be taking them in. They had about six hours before the tide turned. By that time they would either be washed ashore or picked up off the island.

Soon they saw their plywood speedboat floating by. It was upside down, and they couldn't right it, but they grabbed it and hung on. 'There's some flares and a gun in the pocket,' said Jimmy Fraser. If they could get those they could attract attention.

Mike was still wearing the harness he had strapped around his waist when he went forward. He tied it to the timber baulk that was supporting them, then dived under the speedboat, while Robert and Alison hung on to steady it. But their fingers were numb, and every few seconds they were swamped by a wave. They had to keep one hand free to hold on to the beam, and the speedboat slipped away.

Mike came back with two packets of rockets, well waterproofed, but he hadn't been able to find the gun. He handed over the rockets, then swam back to the speedboat, now about 15 yards away, to look for the gun.

The rope was only just long enough. He was underneath the boat for a long time, and he was exhausted when he got back to the beam.

'The gun's gone.'

Without realising how pointless it was, they held on to the flares.

Usually the waves broke right over them, and they were only occasionally carried to the crests. When they were, however, they began to get glimpses of the island. The tide was definitely taking them in.

They were all confident of rescue, and they even made jokes. 'Hope they've got the apple pie on for tonight.' And to Jimmy Fraser, whose thatch was thinning: 'Part your hair in the middle, Uncle Jimmy. Then the helicopter will see your bald head.'

Urged by Jimmy Fraser, they kicked their legs out continually, partly to maintain their circulation and partly in an effort to propel themselves shorewards. But as the light began to fail they grew colder and talked less.

The wreck of the *Mariecelia* had been sighted by now, and the alarm had been raised. But there was no time to organise an air search before dark. The search by cutter and lifeboat, too, was soon abandoned.

The lights of Jersey were tantalisingly close. They could see individual houses, even windows and doors, and once or twice they thought they saw people. But soon the tide would change.

Dolly Fraser, her arm completely numb, was on the verge of collapse. They helped her all they could, but it was becoming plain that she couldn't take much more.

They weren't going to make it on this tide. When Dolly Fraser finally let go, no one spoke. She floated out of reach, and instinctively they shut their minds to it. She had not uttered one word of complaint.

'Alison, have you got a knife?'

The question came from Mike, who was next to Alison on the log. It took her some seconds to digest it. Not so much because it seemed a strange one, but because her mind was as numb as her body.

'No.'

'This rope is slowly dragging me under.'

Mike's voice sounded matter of fact. If there was a note of strain in it she did not detect it.

'What do you mean?'

Slowly, in every really big sea, the beam was revolving. Each time it did so it took another turn of the rope. Mike had tied himself to the beam when he dived under the speedboat, and now their numbed fingers could not untie him.

Alison turned to Robert, who was next to her on her right. 'Mike's in trouble. His rope's getting shorter. Have you got a knife?'

Between getting enough breath to talk, and ducking each wave, that speech took her about a minute.

'No.'

She coiled the rope round her arm and held Mike up.

It seemed that she supported him like that for a long time, the tautened rope biting into her arm. Once, when she looked round, his head was under water.

'Mike, what are you doing?'

With a tremendous effort she pulled him clear. When she stared down into his face she saw that he was dead.

Her basic calm seemed unaffected. It was as though it couldn't really have happened. By collective, tacit agreement they all ignored it. Again, the complete absence of any murmur of complaint obscured the reality.

'I can't hold on any longer.'

The words were spoken by Jimmy Fraser. There was no self-pity in them—it was a simple statement of fact.

'Don't be silly, Dad, hang on a bit longer. They're bound to come for us.'

Jimmy Fraser's injuries had been far more severe than anyone had allowed themselves to imagine. His nose was broken, and he had had difficulty in breathing throughout. He was the next one to let go. Again there was no word of complaint.

Clinging to the beam beside Robert in the darkness, Alison was being continually jostled and bruised by Mike's body to her left. For a long time she hardly noticed it. Then the horror of it penetrated, and she recoiled.

'I can't stand it. He's hitting me all the time.' The seas

were not quite so rough now, the waves less precipitous. 'I'm going to swim for it. It's not that far—I'm sure it's not that far. I can't hang on here any longer. We'll only be taken out to sea again. I'm going to swim for it.'

'I'm with you,' said Robert. 'I'm for it.'

They let go of the beam and struck out for the lights. But Robert lagged behind. 'You must get ashore and tell them what's happened,' she heard him say.

'You must too.'

Away to her left she saw a light dancing on the water. It looked like a buoy. 'Come on, Robert,' she called. 'Let's swim for that buoy.' But Robert didn't answer, and she called again. 'Robert, come on.'

She swam back to look for him, but he was gone. In the space of perhaps half an hour all her friends had died and she was alone.

She imagined that she was somewhere south of La Platte, at the entrance to St. Aubin's Bay, but she sensed, from the continually changing pattern of lights ahead of her, that she was being carried along the coast.

Layers of seaweed were clawing at her, flowing against her, and she knew the tide must have turned. Yet she was no further out from the coast. There was a lighted buoy behind her, and its presence gave her confidence. She was holding her own.

Unknown to her she was being carried eastwards along St. Clement's Bay, leaving St. Helier far to her left. She saw fewer lights now, although sometimes she saw moving splashes of light as cars rounded the headland. She was approaching the south-eastern tip of the island.

The danger now was that she would be carried east of Jersey. But the complex tides and currents typical of the island, coupled with her own tireless efforts, took her round the headland and northwards along Grouville Bay, nearly a mile out but still in sight of the scattered lights on the shore.

1 Captain Gordon Illingworth

2a H.M.S. *Curacoa* in a Norwegian fjord, 1940

2b Stan Farrow, Bob Markham and Harry Bell

Jutting out into the sea to the north was the promontory dominated by Gorey Castle. The pinnacle was floodlit, and it hovered on the cliff-top like a lantern, guiding her path. But despite all her efforts she was unable to get inside the breakwater at the harbour.

For many hours she kept the floodlit castle in view. But now she was looking back at it. She was off St. Catherine's Bay, nearing the north-eastern corner of the island. The lights of the buoys along this stretch of coastline were still to seaward, and she thought she was safe. She was unaware that she was being carried north of the island. The distant lights of the castle were suddenly extinguished, and then the street lights, too, went out. It must be midnight.

The seas were still rough and every time she tried to float she was swamped by them. She had to swim all the time, mostly on her back but almost upright, continually fighting the sea. She could never relax.

Robert's words echoed in her mind throughout the night. She had to get back, to tell them what had happened. It seemed the only important thing. Then she thought of her life, how much she enjoyed everything, how lucky she was, how she would miss it all.

She thought of her birthday presents, and especially of her new car. She didn't want anyone else to have her E-type Jag. That was what would happen if she failed to get back. The thought stimulated her to stay alive.

The darkness was complete now except for a single house in which she could make out the lights of four windows, two upstairs and two down. First the downstairs lights went out, then one of the upstairs, leaving a single light which glowed like a beacon. Then that too was extinguished, leaving a blacked-out coastline.

She was being carried north of the Tour de Rozel now, out to sea. Behind her the northern coastline was receding into the deep niche of Bouley Bay. To seaward, the lights of the buoys had gone. She had lost all sense of orientation, but

D

she knew instinctively that the land was slipping away from her.

Up to this point she had never let herself think that she couldn't make it. But now she felt she couldn't go on. The voices that had urged her not to give up, to get back somehow to tell her story, were silent.

Throughout the night she had been swallowing water as the waves overwhelmed her. Now she began to swallow it purposely. She longed to relax, to sleep, to let the sea have its way. Resigned and acquiescent, luxuriating in the increasing numbness of her mind and body, she was sinking gently when she felt a movement in one of her feet. It was no more than an involuntary twitch, but it roused her to what she was doing. She mustn't give up. Whatever she did she must resist sleep. She began swimming again.

Half-blinded by the salt water, her eyes completely closed, she imagined it was getting light. She heard a seagull, and the plaintive wail of this lone creature warmed and sustained her. Perhaps after all she was not so far from land, and she felt almost happy.

Only a phenomenal natural buoyancy was saving her now. Her efforts at swimming, feeble and mechanical, were scarcely enough to keep her afloat.

The lifeboat was out searching for survivors again, but it was south of the island. To look for anyone to the north would have been absurd—or so it seemed.

She heard a bird singing—a thrush, perhaps, warbling into the teeth of the gale. There was no sign of land, so perhaps there was a fisherman nearby. She would cling to the fisherman's dinghy.

It was fully daylight now, but her eyelids were so swollen she could see very little. Ahead of her she thought she could see a cloud, low down on the water, and she decided to swim for that. But when she looked again it had moved. She was going round in circles.

She seemed to swim towards this cloud for many hours.

She felt she was quite close to it—and then she was conscious of a terrible pounding and roaring. There must be something there, and her arms thrashed the water, desperately, swimming as though in a race.

Suddenly she was grappling with a monster whose teeth were biting into her arms and legs, and into her body. She was being lifted up by the sea and thrown on to some rocks.

During the night the tide had turned again, and instead of being carried out to sea she had drifted right across Bouley Bay. The cloud she had seen was the shoulder of land running northwards to the tip of the island.

For a moment she stood up, then floundered as the sea washed in again. Ahead of her the rocks seemed to rise almost vertically. She dragged herself clear of the water and collapsed.

She had been washed up beneath the highest point of the island, in Petit Port Bay. Half a mile to the north the land ended. Above her the ground rose to 500 feet, with the TV masts that served the island towering at the summit. The coastline itself was rocky, bleak and deserted.

She couldn't stand up, and the wind struck so cold that she rolled back into the water for warmth. Then, forcing her eyes open with her fingers, she scanned the precipices ahead.

She saw what looked like a mountain track. She would follow that. She crawled and stumbled out of the water, learning to walk all over again with each step, slipping back a yard for each two gained. Clinging at first to rocks and boulders, and then to roots and branches, she evolved a method of progress. It began to rain.

She had lost all sense of time and she had no idea how long she climbed, But eventually she reached the top of the cliff. She sat down and rested under a tree. But she was shivering so uncontrollably that she knew she must keep moving.

She started off again along the track, and presently she

heard a dog barking. It was the sweetest sound she had ever heard. The track she was following led into a narrow lane, and she had no sooner entered it than she heard the sound of a car.

What must she look like? The cuts in her head, she could feel, were clotted with blood, her hair was matted and witch-like. When she started swimming she had kicked off her baggy trousers, and all she was wearing was a sweater and panties. Always self-conscious about her weight, she looked down at her legs and saw that they were ugly and swollen from long immersion in the sea.

Not many minutes earlier, vanity would have taken second place to self-preservation; but now vanity won. She dived into the bracken.

When the car had gone she heard the dog again. Soon afterwards, following the sound, she staggered into the yard of Lower Egypt Farm. To farmer William de la Mare and his sons she was an apparition. Her head was enlarged, the contours of her face were flattened with swelling, her eyes had disappeared, and her neck was inflated to twice its normal size, so that a pendant she was wearing had to be cut off. Her body was bloated, her arms and legs distended, and the cuts from flying glass and the abrasions from the rocks had torn and shredded her skin and streaked it with blood. She was jabbering hysterically, and it was several minutes before she could talk coherently. Then the story she was burning to tell poured out.

When she stumbled into the farmyard the time was 11.30 on the morning of 10th October. After being in the water for 20 hours, she had found her own way to safety.

* * *

Alison Mitchell recovered completely from her ordeal, and two years later she married. Today she is the mother of two young children. Slim and slender compared with the plump girl of eight years ago, she knows it was largely because of that plumpness that she escaped with her life.

Her 21st birthday party seems incredibly distant, the details blurred by the tragic events which followed. Her most poignant memory of that party is of Robert Fraser inventing a new dance and teaching her the steps—or rather the strokes. It was a combination of many familiar arm and leg movements, and he called it 'The Swim'.

3

The Jeanne Gougy

Coastguardsman Desmond Winchester, the watchman in the lookout hut on Cape Cornwall, had been on duty since midnight. The lookout hut faced westwards, straight out at the Atlantic, and the gales and storms of a typical November night—the year was 1962—had not yet blown themselves out. For a time, indeed, it had seemed as though the wind that rattled the wide bay windows of the tiny wooden hut high on the promontory would tear it off its perch. Driving rain had reduced visibility to almost nothing, so that even the Brisons, the group of rocks half a mile off the Cape, had disappeared from view. But by four o'clock the rain had ceased and visibility began to improve.

To Winchester's right the rugged coastline curved north-eastwards towards St. Ives and Newquay, cutting off any view of the land. To his left the big sweep of Whitesands Bay was similarly cut off, but on the far side of the bay, $3\frac{1}{2}$ miles across the water, the dark outline of the cliff-top was now faintly visible as it climbed above Sennen Cove and rose to the final abrupt solitude of Land's End. And off Land's End he could see the red glow of the lighthouse on the Longships, warning mariners of the treacherous rocks.

The small shaded working light under which Winchester made up his log was switched off and he stood there in darkness, staring into darkness. Yet to his accustomed night vision the blackness had become a gradation of greys and indigos, each tiny gradation marking some recognisable feature. Half-way up his window the gun-metal sea became a blur, then lifted almost imperceptibly into a leaden sky. The black humps of the Brisons were pushing up now through the darkness. And at the foot of the Cape there was a glow of phosphorescence where the sea pounded with angry roar on the outlying rocks, sometimes projecting a tiny waterspout of spray 150 feet up against the windows of the hut.

Half-right, in the direction of Southern Ireland, Winchester could make out a dim red light, and he reached for his binoculars. It was the port light of a ship, about three miles off the coast, steaming south. The vessel was crossing in front of Cape Cornwall on a course which Winchester estimated would take her through the safe channel between the Longships and Land's End. He noticed, though, that she was unusually close to the Brisons. He would have to keep an eye on her.

The vessel was the 273-ton Dieppe trawler *Jeanne Gougy*.

In the next few minutes, as the vessel crossed Whitesands Bay, it seemed to Winchester that she was making her approach much too close to the Land's End side of the channel. She almost seemed to be steering for the tip of Land's End itself. He picked up his signalling lamp and went outside on to the narrow platform that surrounded the hut, steadying himself on the iron railing. From there, almost blown off his feet by the gale, he flashed a succession of warnings to the unknown vessel. 'You are standing into danger,' was the literal translation of the signal. But there was no response from the trawler.

There were 18 men on the *Jeanne Gougy*. Fifteen of them were sleeping in the cabins down in the forecastle. The other three were on watch in the wheelhouse. Master of the trawler was 40-year-old Joseph Penher, who had the reputation of being one of the best captains in Dieppe. His ship was the largest of the local trawler fleet. His chief engineer, Jean Grizard, father of six, had worked for the same fleet for 12 years.

Oldest man in the crew was 52-year-old Victor David, already twice shipwrecked. 'Jamais deux sans trois' was his favourite saying—'Never two without three'. Tonight he was asleep in the forecastle. Jean-Claude Poussin, the cook, was at sea for the first time. Previously he had worked in hotels. Michel Pade, fair and blue-eyed, with small moustache and trimmed beard, was getting married at the end of the trip to dark-haired Colette Heitz. He too was in the forecastle. Youngest on board was the 16-year-old cabin boy Jean Ridel. He had been at sea for three months and this was his third trip in the *Jeanne Gougy*.

The trawler had been at sea for 10 days, and for most of that time the crew had been hard at work 18 hours a day, putting down the nets and bringing them up every two hours. They were approaching the limits of fatigue. Then, homeward bound from their fishing grounds off Southern Ireland, they had run into some of the worst weather they had ever known. First the lightning had illuminated the mountainous seas and scurrying cloud, then deafening explosions of thunder had split the heavens and made way for torrential rain. As the trawler danced to the cacophony of the tempest, the tired Dieppe seamen slipped from fatigue to exhaustion.

When at last the worst furies of the storm were spent, the men on watch inevitably relaxed; as the trawler ploughed through the heavy swell towards Land's End and the English Channel, the worst of the voyage over, their lids grew heavy. One by one they dozed until, passing Cape Cornwall and beginning the crossing of Whitesands Bay, not a single man was properly awake. Thus, as Coastguardsman Winchester transmitted his warning signals, no one on board the vessel saw the flashing light.

It seemed to Winchester, shortly after he flashed his lamp, that the vessel turned to port as though making for Sennen Cove. He could see the masthead light standing out against the cliff background. But suddenly he was aware that the light was stationary. For some reason the vessel had stopped. Its behaviour was puzzling, and Winchester put a call through to the auxiliary coastguard at Sennen, asking him to man the hut on the cliffs above the cove. The time was 05.12.

One minute earlier, at 05.11, Land's End radio had picked up an S.O.S. *'M'Aidez, M'Aidez. Ashore on Longships, require immediate assistance.'* The call-sign was that of the *Jeanne Gougy.*

In fact the vessel was not on the Longships at all. After striking a submerged reef which tore a hole in her hull, she had driven on into a deep niche in the cliff-face, 200 feet below the First and Last House, right on the tip of Land's End.

A single red distress flare rocketed lazily into the night, lighting up the coastline. Coastguardsman Winchester hurried out on to the platform and acknowledged it with a white recognition signal. Then the darkness was complete. Even the ship's lights had gone out. Winchester went back into his hut and picked up the phone.

First he rang 'Father' Bridger, the 63-year-old Coastguard District Officer, veteran of scores of rescues, whose name was a byword on the Cornish coast. White-haired but fearless, Bridger had served for 25 years as a Yeoman of Signals in the Royal Navy and followed it with 23 years in the coastguard service. 'Call out the St. Just and Sennen lifesaving companies,' ordered Bridger, 'and advise Sennen lifeboat to launch. I'm going straight to the casualty.' Within two minutes, maroons were being fired at St. Just and Sennen to call out the volunteers. Three minutes later the Sennen lifeboat was being launched.

The *Jeanne Gougy*, rammed hard on the rocks, was tipping over on to her port side. Heavy seas were breaking over the wheelhouse and the cabins were flooding rapidly. The 15 men in the forecastle sprang from their bunks. Within a minute the water was up to their necks.

Six of the men in the forward cabins managed to bunch together, but they could see nothing of their comrades, whom they feared must all have been drowned. Michel Pade addressed the remainder. 'Come on, boys—our only chance is to get across the deck to the wheelhouse. We must be quick.'

'Michel, you're crazy.' It was Captain Penher speaking. 'We'll never get there. We'll be carried away by the waves.' Nevertheless, led by Michel Pade, the six men climbed out of the forecastle and chose a moment between the assaults of the sea to begin their scramble across the slanting deck, flattening themselves against first one object and then another as the waves broke over the vessel. Among them, in addition to Captain Penher, were the chief engineer, the cook, and the cabin-boy.

It was at this moment, as the six seamen played touch with the swell in a desperate effort to gain the wheelhouse, that District Officer Bridger and three coastguard men reached the First and Last House and began descending the cliff, guided by the stench of oil and the shouts of the men exposed on deck. The grass at the top of the slope was steep and slippery, but at last they reached a rocky ledge 70 feet above the sea, from where the cliff dropped absolutely sheer. There below them, lying helplessly on its side, twitching like an animal in its death-throes, lay the *Jeanne Gougy*.

It seemed to Bridger and the other coastguard men, in the fierce light shed by their portable floodlight, that the deck of the vessel was swarming with life. As the six seamen flitted from one handhold to another between the swell they seemed to multiply themselves fourfold. But at length all six men reached the shelter of the wheelhouse and disappeared inside. As they did so a huge curling wave submerged the bridge completely; but just when it seemed to the seamen that they were trapped the sea washed back and left them with a few feet of breathing space.

There was no one else in the neighbourhood of the wheelhouse. The three men on watch, it seemed, had been washed away.

Five more men had already succumbed in the waterlogged

forecastle. Four others, crowded together in a tiny air lock, were struggling to keep alive. Veteran seaman Victor David was among them. 'Come close to me,' shouted David, 'we must hold on to each other.' And the other three—two youths of 18 and a man of 42—clung to him in a tiny sanctuary measuring less than a square yard, lifted off their feet many times by the rising water but not quite overwhelmed. Above them the porthole in the starboard side of the ship was almost continually awash, but somehow the air-lock held. There was no way out except through that port-hole. They had no alternative but to stay where they were and hope to survive until the ebb tide.

The fact that there were four men still alive in the fore-peak was unknown to the rescuers on the cliff ledge, and also to the men in the wheelhouse, who believed themselves to be the only survivors. The tide was rising, and Bridger was determined to make contact with these men. First he fired a flare, in the light of which he could see the full outline of the ship. It had an 80-degree list now and for four-fifths of the time was completely submerged. Only as the seas washed off was the deckhouse visible. Also in the light of the flare he could see the Sennen lifeboat, standing off beyond the rocks, unable to approach within 100 yards of the wreck.

He fired a rocket line across the ship and it fell three feet in front of the wheelhouse, but no one grabbed it. The starboard door of the wheelhouse was almost horizontal, and Bridger guessed that it must be difficult to open from the inside. He fired another line and this time landed it right across the wheelhouse. In the trough of the swell an arm appeared from the centre window and groped but failed to grip. The next moment the ship was submerged again.

Bridger sent up another flare and then fired a third line. This time it landed right outside the wheelhouse door. He could still hear cries coming from the wheelhouse and knew that there must be survivors there. He waited a few seconds, then called the cliff-top on his walkie-talkie radio. 'Send for the R.A.F. helicopter,' he said. 'When the tide goes down they may be able to put a man aboard.'

Suddenly the wheelhouse door swung open, and quickly Bridger sent up another flare. One of the crew crawled outside the door and grabbed the line. A cheer went up from the men on the cliff—and then as suddenly died away. A huge sea broke over the wheelhouse in that moment, and as it sucked back in a powerful waterfall the watchers saw with dismay that the man had disappeared. The wheelhouse door, too, had gone, wrenched off at the hinges by the crushing weight of the sea.

As the *Jeanne Gougy* threw off this great load of water before cowering again beneath the next wave, Bridger saw five men being swept through the wheelhouse like flotsam. When the sea receded they too had disappeared.

All was silent now in the wheelhouse. The efforts to save life had seemingly done no more than hasten its end. The tide was full and the ship could be glimpsed only momentarily, well beneath the surface. Meanwhile the life-saving companies had arrived, and they manhandled their heavy apparatus down to the ledge, but it seemed they would not be needed. The rescue party, consisting in all of about 25 men, stared down gloomily at the submerged wreck.

One man alone still hoped. District Officer Bridger had brought off too many miraculous rescues to give up altogether. He fired another line, but all he could hear in reply was the eerie ringing of the ship's bell as the vessel shifted and settled still more deeply on the rocky bottom.

When daylight came the lifeboat was still off Land's End, unable to approach any closer. An R.A.F. helicopter, too, had arrived and was manoeuvring off the coast, getting into position for a close-up view. The pilot, Flight Lieutenant Trevor Egginton, was too preoccupied in holding his position in the high winds for more than a cursory look, but Flight Lieutenant Jack Canham, navigator, and Sergeant Eric Smith, winchman, were staring down at the wreck.

There was no sign of life on board, and the ship was still being continually covered by the swell. It looked impossible for anyone to be alive down there. Egginton pulled up, crossed the coastline and landed on top of the cliff, where he talked to members of the coastguard. Bridger sent him a message asking him to do a search of the area, and soon the helicopter took off again and flew out to sea, then began to sweep along the coast.

Debris from the wreck was already littering the coastline. Nets, deck cargo, a length of tarpaulin, splintered blocks of wood, a hatch covering—all had presumably come from the *Jeanne Gougy*. Then Egginton spotted a man in the water. He put a smoke float down to mark the spot, then descended towards it.

'He looks dead,' said winchman Eric Smith.

'You can't guarantee it,' said Egginton.

Smith, of medium height, dark-haired and boyish, connected up his harness, and while Canham operated the winch Smith went down on the cable. The man in the water was wearing a lifejacket, and this made it difficult for Smith to get the rescue belt under his arms. The man was limp and lifeless, and Smith thought he was probably dead, but he finally secured the man in the harness and motioned to Canham to haul the two of them up. Between them Canham and Smith used oxygen equipment and artificial respiration to try to bring the man round, but there was no response. They landed on a sports field at Penzance, from where the man was rushed to hospital, but they had been too late.

Meanwhile the lifeboat had picked up two more bodies. The fate of the crew of the *Jeanne Gougy* now seemed settled beyond all reasonable doubt.

The helicopter, short of fuel, went on to Culdrose. On the cliff-top Bridger addressed the life-saving companies. He could not keep them on voluntary duty indefinitely. 'Is there anyone who has urgent business to attend to?' No one moved, and Bridger continued: 'I've laid on refreshments for you at the Land's End Hotel. Half of you can go now, the other half later. But I feel there's still a chance we might find someone alive on board. So I've kept all the equipment ready, with cliff ladders in position and cliff lines rigged. I intend to make an attempt to board her myself at low water—that's soon after midday. I'm not giving up all hope yet.' He was the only one who hadn't.

Sightseers from all over Cornwall were crowding on to the cliff-top and special police were drafted in to keep them back. The sea was still washing over the wreck, obliterating it for much of the time, and it was not until after 11.30 that the tide ebbed sufficiently for anyone on the cliff to get a prolonged look at the ship. There was no movement of any kind from inside the wheelhouse. The deck, or what they could see of it with the ship turned away from them on its side, had been swept almost clean. The task of the boarding party looked formidable—and unrewarding.

Bridger had hardly taken his eyes off the wreck for six hours. Now he was staring into the wheelhouse through field-glasses, trying to make out some detail. Hundreds of sightseers on the cliff-top were similarly staring down. Suddenly it seemed to the watchers that a face appeared momentarily in the middle window of the wheelhouse.

'There's a man!'

The image was gone—yet it was imprinted indelibly on too many minds for it to have been hallucination. Without doubt there had been a face there—fair-haired, bearded, haggard, pale.

'Fire!'

The order came from Bridger a second later. The rescue rocket sped over the hull and landed by the wheelhouse door. Then, amid gasps of astonishment and an emotional cheer from the cliff, a man's hand appeared and groped for the line. The man was Michel Pade, the blue-eyed French fisherman whose fiancée Colette was already red-eyed with grief in Dieppe. Somehow this man had lived virtually under water for more than six hours.

Bridger put another call through on his radio. 'Get the helicopter back. Tell them there's a survivor in the wheelhouse. They may have to go down and get him.'

Again and again, as the sea swept over the ship, Michel Pade had held his breath for upwards of half a minute, completely submerged. One by one he had watched his comrades die. As they became more and more exhausted by their efforts to get enough air to stay alive, they had reached a stage where they didn't know what they were doing. Sometimes they had held their breath when the water receded and inhaled when they were submerged. They had come up gasping and choking—and soon they had not come up at all. The cabin-boy had simply disappeared, and he had watched the last struggle of the cook, the chief engineer and the captain without being able to help. Their agony had been terrible to see. With every new giant wave that engulfed them, Michel Pade had expected it to be his turn to die.

Now, with a superhuman effort, Pade hauled on the line. Attached to it was the rope and tackle of the breeches buoy, heavy and cumbersome, normally the work of two or more men to haul in and secure. And the rope was fouling one of the mast stay-wires, making the task doubly difficult. Even now, although the tide was ebbing, the sea was breaking heavily over the wheelhouse. Yet the exhausted Pade finally managed it, securing the rope to the centre strut of the wheelhouse window. Then the man on the ledge began hauling out the breeches buoy.

Soon the lifebelt had been pulled right to the foot of the wheelhouse door. But Michel Pade, exhausted by his efforts and by the long hours of immersion and exposure, still clung to the wheelhouse window. He was too weak to reach the breeches buoy. It was as well that Bridger had sent for the helicopter. And in the next minute they heard it and saw it as it flew over the coast from inland.

It was as they were standing there staring up at the helicopter and pointing down at the wheelhouse that an incredible thing happened. No one could quite grasp its meaning for a moment. Four men had appeared as if from nowhere and were scrambling over the rail in the bows. It hardly seemed that they could have come from inside the ship. Yet it had been impossible to put down a boarding party, and the lifeboat was still beyond Land's End. The men must have come from the submerged forecastle.

Victor David and his party, immured up in the forepeak, had somehow kept their faces above water hour after hour, clinging to each other, urged on all the time by David himself. When at last the tide ebbed and the sea became less violent and the ship more stable, they decided to take their chance, and they had crawled out through the porthole and climbed up to the rail. They had seen the helicopter fly over nearly four hours earlier, but they had believed they were on the Longships and they were amazed when they found they were right up against the cliffs of Land's End.

In the wheelhouse, Michel Pade was as astonished as anyone. He waved towards the four men and pointed to the breeches buoy. But soon afterwards he collapsed back into the wheelhouse and disappeared from view. Bridger decided to get the men off the forepeak with the breeches buoy and leave the man in the wheelhouse to the helicopter. Under his direction, the men of the life-saving companies were already hauling the buoy back along the rope, trying to manoeuvre it into position over the rail in the bows.

Meanwhile Flight Lieutenant Egginton was making a practice run in the helicopter. Looking down from the open helicopter door, winchman Eric Smith could see that the wreck was still being continually swamped by the swell. In these conditions he could easily be swept off his feet. Then, if the cable fouled some obstruction, there would be two men trapped instead of one. It didn't look like a job for a winchman, and Smith didn't fancy it at all. The best course

3a Alain Bombard

3b Alison Mitchell
in hospital
after her ordeal

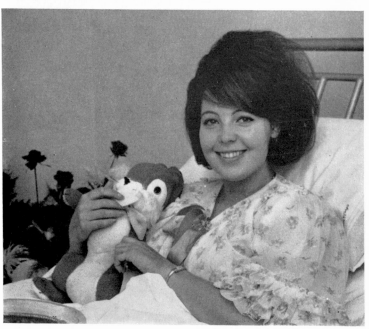

4 Sergeant Eric Smith being winched down
to the *Jeanne Gougy*

seemed to be to lower the strop to the wheelhouse and let the man fit it himself—assuming he was capable of doing so.

Up in the cockpit, Egginton could see ahead but not underneath. Guided by Canham, who was looking down from the side door, he began his final run towards the cliff, reducing speed as he did so. Canham began the count-down, calling at 20 yards, then 10 yards, and finally yard by yard. Egginton, flying at 60 feet, brought the helicopter closer and closer to the cliff. The ledge on which the coastguards stood was just above eye level, and the cliff itself towered above them. The ship was so embedded in the rock fissure that the rotor blades were desperately near the cliff. The smallest error of judgment would be fatal for them all.

The wind that swept towards them over the top of the cliff was bringing with it an unpredictable turbulence and down-draught, liable to fluctuate. A cross-wind was feeding in to the area round the corner of Land's End, buffeting the heli-copter sideways, increasing the danger of smashing those whirling rotor blades into the craggy chunk of rock that faced them. The swell was still exploding at the foot of the cliffs and across the wreck, throwing up showers of spray which were picked up and diffused by the rotor blades. Egg-inton had his windscreen wipers on but the spray was salt and sticky and the windows soon misted up.

It was essential to hover into wind, and that, as it hap-pened, meant facing dead into the sun. The light was fierce, almost blinding, and Egginton focused on the white skull-cap of one of the coastguards on the ledge, keeping that as a reference point. All the time Canham was guiding him on the inter-com.

'Three yards. Two yards. One yard.' And then— 'Steady.'

Canham had already lowered the strop and it was touching the wheelhouse. No one emerged to grab hold of it. It seemed after all that Smith would have to go down. Canham wound up the cable while Smith explained the

E

situation to Egginton. 'All right,' said Egginton, 'you'll have
to go down. But you're not to come off the cable. That's an
order.'

Egginton backed the helicopter away from the cliff in
preparation for another approach. Smith, sitting on the edge
of the door with his legs dangling, looked down at the point
he had to reach. He was an experienced enough winchman
to know that he was going to be frightened.

No matter how many times you went down on the cable, it
remained an unnatural thing to do. You knew you were
risking your neck. For Smith it was the same sort of feeling
that car-drivers had when they were overtaking another car
and weren't quite sure they were going to make it. His heart-
beat went up, his diaphragm contracted, his breathing
became shallow. He had to take several deep breaths to settle
his nerves. Yet with it he got a heightened sense of per-
ception. All he had ever learned in the way of airmanship
was suddenly at his fingertips.

'Winching out.'

They were about 50 yards from the wreck and Canham
had begun to lower him away. He dangled for a moment at
the door, then his intercom plug was dragged out by his own
weight as he swung down.

He was on his own now. Soon he forgot that he was hanging by a wire from a helicopter. All his thoughts were concentrated into what lay below him. He took in the cluster of
men on the ledge, saw that the breeches buoy had been
rigged and that the first man from the forepeak was already
suspended in mid-air, half-way across. A long swell was still
hitting the side of the ship and throwing huge waterfalls
across the wheelhouse, and this scared him, so he decided not
to look at it. Below him there seemed to be a mass of nets,
ropes, masts and patches of oil, tossed into confusion by the
green foaming water. Any one of several obstructions could
foul the cable and prevent his return to the helicopter. He
decided not to look at them either.

He was in the shelter of the cliff now and the turbulence was reduced, but the cable was oscillating and as he descended he swung too far, beyond and above the wheelhouse. He grabbed the rail—and held on in spite of the shock of static electricity that passed through him. Then an enormous sea hit him. Somehow he ducked into it and held on.

He did not look up at the helicopter. Aeroplanes had been known to fail, but if he thought about that he would never do his job. He climbed along the superstructure to the door of the wheelhouse and peered inside. It was waterlogged and empty. What could have happened to the man they had seen? Could he have drowned in the last few minutes? Halfway across the wheelhouse Smith could see the entrance to a passage-way or corridor. Perhaps the man was sheltering there.

The watchers on the cliff saw the winchman disappear into the wheelhouse. A moment later another huge sea broke over the ship. Taken by surprise, Smith swallowed a mouthful of oily sea-water and nearly choked. Recovering, he shuffled along towards the corridor. There, pale, wet and bedraggled, passive and silent, was the bearded Frenchman Michel Pade. He was staring at Smith uncomprehendingly, as though he simply wasn't there.

Behind Pade, in the shadows of the corridor, lurked another slumped, sodden figure. Smith didn't know whether he was alive or dead. He showed no animation, but when Smith looked at him more closely he noticed a tiny flicker in his stare. It was the 16-year-old cabin-boy Jean Ridel, miraculously still alive.

Smith had expected to have to struggle to get the man into the strop, but he was completely limp. He didn't hinder—but he didn't help. Smith had to do everything for him—fit him into the strop, then find the leverage to drag him out of the wheelhouse. At last he had him balanced on the edge of the door, his head outside, his body in. Then he gave the thumbs up to Canham.

As the cable began to tauten, Smith shouted back into the wheelhouse at the cabin boy. 'I'll come back for you in a minute.' The boy did not answer.

They were clear of obstruction and the winch slowly pulled them up. When they were both safely aboard, Egginton climbed and turned away before coming in over the cliff and landing by the First and Last House. They off-loaded Pade, then took off again to get Ridel.

Meanwhile the life-saving teams, balanced precariously on the ledge, unable to drive in their stake supports because of the solid rock they were standing on, were lifting the four men on the forepeak across the rocks virtually by hand. One half of the company supported the weight while the other half hauled in the buoy. One slip on the ledge, one weakness in the chain, and the man in the buoy would have fallen to his death, dragging with him several of the men on the ledge. But as the helicopter went back for the second time, the fourth man on the forepeak was brought safely ashore.

The tension and risk of the rescue of Michel Pade was duplicated in the next few minutes as Egginton held the helicopter in position under the cliff and Smith went down again on the cable. Eventually Jean Ridel was safely brought out. How he had survived in that narrow passage-way for nearly eight hours, continually swamped by the influx of water, remained a mystery. Indeed his survival suggested that there might be others still alive somewhere in the hull. So twice more, after the rescue of the cabin boy, Eric Smith went back and searched the ship, crawling once more into the narrow passage and shouting but hearing no answer, then going down again and peering through every porthole and hatch that wasn't under water. But there was no further sign of life.

Back on the cliff-top, District Officer Bridger asked the helicopter crew to do one more sweep of the area, just to make sure there was no one still alive in the water. Down the coast they found yet another body, and as Smith looked down at it, all the nausea of the last few hours—the tension, the fear, the immersion, the physical effort, the confinement in that narrow corridor, the oily water in his lungs—suddenly swept over him. After his fourth descent to the wreck he had thought his work was over, and he had relaxed. He feared that if he went down now for this last body, naked and macabre in the water, he would almost certainly pass out.

As he moved wearily towards the harness he was intercepted by the navigator, Jack Canham. Canham was on his first helicopter rescue, but he was an experienced operational flyer, and he knew when a man's reserves were spent. Quietly but firmly, he took the harness from Eric Smith and went down in his place.

* * *

Flight Lieutenant John Trevor Egginton is now a Rotary Wing Tutor at the Empire Test Pilots' School at Boscombe Down. Like the rest of the helicopter crew he was awarded the Chevalier du Mérite Maritime by the French—and granted unrestricted permission by the Queen to wear the decoration. In 1964 he was awarded the Air Force Cross. Eric Smith, who left the Service in 1965, was awarded the George Medal for his work in this rescue. Jack Canham, who won a wartime D.F.C. with Bomber Command before being taken prisoner in 1943, was killed in an accident to a Whirlwind helicopter in September 1965. He was 44.

District Officer W. J. Bridger retired from H. M. Coastguard Service in 1964.

4

Alain Bombard

The rotund little house surgeon at the hospital at Boulogne was a man with heretical ideas. Hirsute and dynamic, with unruly black hair and flashing brown eyes, he was a 26-year-old rebel whose theories clashed with all past medical experience and teaching. His name was Alain Bombard.

For centuries man had regarded the oceans as inimical. The literature of many races had testified again and again to the cold dispassionate cruelty of the sea. Many thousands of seamen had perished in storm and tempest or died a lingering death from thirst and exposure, and one of the great tragic figures of the 19th and 20th centuries had been the shipwrecked mariner, clinging to a life-raft, despairing of rescue, waiting for the last agonised tortures of madness and thirst. But in 1953 the Frenchman Bombard put the proposition to an incredulous world that the sea could provide the basic needs of human life as readily as the land: fats, proteins, carbohydrates, vitamins, and—the ultimate heresy—abundant water.

It took, recalled Bombard, about a month to die of starvation and about ten days to die of thirst. Yet most castaways died within three days. Haunted by the spectre of hunger and thirst, believing death to be inevitable, they quickly succumbed to despair. Bombard believed that this spectre was a hallucination born of ignorance. He proposed to prove that in these apparently hopeless conditions, alone on a tiny raft in mid-ocean without food or water, it was possible to prolong life indefinitely.

All the established authorities on survival at sea agreed that to drink sea-water was to hasten death. The human organism was not suited to such a high salt intake. Nephritis—inflammation of the kidneys—quickly resulted. Such authorities pointed to the experience of many shipwrecked parties, in which, even when they survived, the people who drank sea-water were always in far worse condition than those who abstained.

Bombard believed that most shipwrecked seamen drank sea-water only as a last resort, when their bodies were already dehydrated and their thirst raging. The sudden intake of salt was generally fatal. He did not dispute that the drinking of sea-water was dangerous, but he held that if the intake was carefully controlled it could sustain the castaway over the first critical days following shipwreck, after which other sources of liquid might be found.

He believed, too, that the knowledge that sea-water could be drunk safely for limited periods, confirmed by scientific experiment, would have an immense psychological effect on the mind of the castaway.

For his other, more permanent sources of liquid Bombard looked to rain-water, which fell at varying intervals in most ocean areas, and to the natural moisture secreted in all fish. After an incision was made in the carcase of fish, water—fresh water—soon drained into the wound. A better method was to squeeze the moisture out by the use of a press, but either method would produce fresh water. So the pattern Bombard envisaged for the preservation of life was, first, the sea, which he believed could be drunk at the rate of not more than $1\frac{1}{2}$ pints a day for five to seven days; second, the moisture contained in fish, which would be available after the first few days; and third, the long-term collection of rain-water. One good rainfall would provide enough fresh water for a month.

There remained the problem of a balanced diet. Bombard was not convinced by warnings that fish might be non-existent and anyway difficult to catch. Again the danger period, he felt, would be the first few days after shipwreck. Once the raft had become a familiar object it would be surrounded by fish. They could then be speared or hooked quite easily.

Fats, proteins and nearly all the vitamins were present in fish. There remained one important deficiency—Vitamin C, present only in fresh fruit and vegetables. A diet without Vitamin C bred scurvy, the traditional scourge of the sailor. Yet Bombard had an answer even to this. He believed that the sea provided its own remedy in the form of plankton.

Plankton was the name given to the microscopic vegetable and animal organisms suspended near the surface of the sea. The whale, the biggest mammal, needed Vitamin C, yet it grew to a weight of 50 tons, mostly on plankton. The obvious inference was that plankton contained the missing vitamin. Bombard proceeded to verify this by scientific analysis.

He soon found that the gathering of these minute substances was a simple matter. Even a shirt trailed in the water accumulated about three ounces of plankton in two hours, rich in calories and more than enough for a day's supply.

Although he was a scientist, Bombard was also a man of practical and physical achievement. He had twice attempted to swim the Channel, giving up the second time after 12 hours in the water. His aim now was not merely to convince a few scientists of the validity of his theories; he saw his experiments as having a much wider application than that. He wanted to prove that victims of shipwreck could survive at sea indefinitely if they followed a few simple rules. Bombard was a romantic, and the plight of the castaway held a special fascination for him. Proof in the laboratory, he knew, would never convince hardened seamen. He would have to demonstrate it on the ocean, exalting the experiment into terms of human endeavour, another step forward in man's conquest of the seas.

It was here that he parted company with the scientists. They at once dismissed him as a stunt man. Prejudice against his revolutionary theories widened and he was held up to ridicule as the mad doctor of Boulogne. Yet he persuaded a Dutch manufacturer of life-saving equipment to finance his research, and it was agreed that an attempt should be made to cross the Atlantic in a small raft. The party was to consist of three men, one of them a navigator—Bombard had not contemplated making the experiment alone. But when faced with the reality of drinking sea-water to survive the other possible starters dropped out one by one. A preliminary experiment in the Mediterranean, in which Bombard and a companion accepted food and water from a passing ship, brought disillusion to Bombard's backers and calumny and derision to Bombard. It became plain that of all the people who knew of his theories and plans, only Bombard himself genuinely believed in them.

Thus it was that, on Sunday 19th October 1953, a horseshoe-shaped inflatable raft, 15 feet long and 6 feet wide, aptly named *L'Hérétique*, sailed westwards from the Canaries with a lone pioneer, unskilled and unpractised in navigation, in defiance of the persuasive coaxings of former supporters and friends and the sepulchral warnings of science and medicine.

The first warning was that the tiny dinghy would be overwhelmed by the first really big sea. In any case it would be impossible to steer. Bombard would be becalmed in the doldrums or enmeshed in the choking seaweed of the Sargasso Sea. Great areas of ocean were barren and sterile; he would find no fish in mid-Atlantic. His proposed diet contained serious deficiencies and if he persisted in his plan to drink sea-water it would kill him. Unlike the Mediterranean, said the cynics, there would be no ships in mid-Atlantic to come to his aid when things went wrong.

For all his past setbacks, Bombard retained an unshakable belief in his theories. To support them he had his missionary zeal, the ideal of a unique and valuable service to mankind. This fortified him against the doubters and against his own natural fears, aggravated as they were by the knowledge that he was leaving his wife Ginette and their three children, including a new-born baby. It was true enough that there might be weaknesses in his theories. Only this experiment, in combat with a great ocean—though Bombard preferred to think of it as in co-operation—could thoroughly probe the theory and convince the sceptics.

Bombard planned to sail south-south-west until he was off the Cape Verde Islands, about latitude 20 North, then west across the Atlantic. This, he hoped, would take him well to the south of the doldrums and the choking seaweed of the Sargasso Sea. He had sailed alone in *L'Hérétique* from Tangier to Las Palmas, and although this had been little more than a coast-crawl it had given him confidence in his ability to steer a course and reach a destination.

Before his departure from Las Palmas the French authorities insisted that he carry a small store of emergency food, equipment and water. Bombard objected, but sailing permission was made dependent upon his accepting it. The equipment, in fact, was no more than he might expect to find in any lifeboat. The food and water were carefully sealed.

The moment of departure had a chilling finality about it. There could be no turning back. The dinghy, its mast mounted well forward, could not sail into wind. The trade wind that he relied on to get him across the Atlantic would just as surely prevent him from putting back. He was committed.

But the beginning at least seemed auspicious. It was a fine clear day, the wind blew strongly, and the little dinghy hurried along at more than three knots. It was not until the evening, when the wind dropped, that Bombard felt any misgivings. He had seen no fish all day.

Next day there was still no wind. A few small pilot fish swam ahead of the dinghy, but there was nothing big enough to provide food or water. Nor did he have any means of catching the smaller fish. He had no nets or lines, and had provided himself with nothing more than a castaway might reasonably hope to possess—a necktie, shoelaces, a strand of rope, a penknife. When larger fish appeared he hoped to spear them with his knife.

But still the waters were empty of fish. And still there was no wind. The absence of any breeze made it unbearably hot, and he was tormented by thirst. On the morning of the third day he began to drink sea-water.

When the wind came that night it quickly stiffened into a gale. Bombard, trying to sleep, suddenly found himself swimming frantically, as though waking from a nightmare. A giant wave had crashed over the dinghy, flooding it so badly that for a moment Bombard was completely submerged. The waterlogged dinghy continued to wallow along soggily before the wind. In minutes, it seemed, the dinghy would be a wreck, torn to shreds by the weight of water. Desperately Bombard began baling, scooping up the water first with his cupped hands and then with his hat. For a long time he seemed to make no progress, but at the end of two hours, exhausted and shivering with cold, he had the dinghy seaworthy again.

At dawn he found that he was still in sight of land. If this was to be his experience in coastal waters, what sort of seas might he meet later on?

The following night he lowered the sail before going to sleep, and trailed the sea anchor, a drogue-like brake which kept the dinghy heading into the swell. It meant sacrificing progress, but this was better than being swamped a second time. He was still drinking sea-water.

The wind was strong next day, but another disaster overtook him when the sail, carefully trimmed to the wind, tore right across the middle. He had a spare sail and he hoisted it, wondering as he did so whether this was quite playing to the rules of shipwreck. But whatever his scruples they were soon literally swept away. A terrific gust of wind caught the new sail and ripped it away like washing off a line.

Bombard watched it skimming the surface of the sea like a spilled parachute a quarter of a mile away, quite irrecoverable. He set to work with needle and thread to repair the old sail, feeling more than ever like a true castaway. His needlework had to be good; that torn sail had to get him across the Atlantic. From this point on, every time he saw the sail billowing he thought of his intricate but amateurish stitching and wondered if it would hold.

The incident effected the first breach in his morale. Cold and hungry, uncertain of his progress, still forced to drink sea-water, he began to doubt whether his equipment—even the dinghy itself—would stand the strain. He had not expected to have these nagging worries about his equipment. He had regarded the dinghy as safe, indestructible. He was prepared for some deterioration in his body, and this had seemed the greatest threat. But now, obsessed with fears and imaginings about his equipment, consumed with doubts about his position, he saw that his main struggle for survival would lie, as with most castaways, not in the body but in the mind.

It was on the sixth day that the fish began to appear. At first they approached the dinghy suspiciously and mostly kept their distance, scattering immediately when he took notice of them. But they would get used to him soon. He began to fashion a harpoon out of his penknife, bending the point on the flat of an oar, pressing firmly but cautiously, careful not to snap the blade. He then lashed the handle of the knife to the end of an oar. Now he had his harpoon.

His first efforts at spearing the fish failed. Several times he felt the blade sink into flesh, but each time the fish shook themselves violently and wriggled away, discolouring the water with their blood. He examined the lashing fearfully after each attempt, terrified of losing the precious blade. The seventh day came, and still he was existing on sea-water.

Each day he made up his log. Even if he did not himself survive, there was the chance that the dinghy might float and the log be preserved. Already he had proved that a man could live for a week on sea-water alone and be comparatively fit at the end of it. It was a depressing thought that this triumph might never be known.

It was on the seventh day that he caught his first fish.

It was a good-sized dolphin, yielding everything he needed—food, water, bait, even a bone behind the gills shaped in the form of a fish-hook. He believed now that he would have no more worries about food or water for the rest of the voyage. What did concern him though was his calculation of position. The height of the sun above the horizon at noon determined his latitude, and the changing time by the sun gave him his longitude. But ten days out he broke his watch-strap, and soon afterwards his watch stopped. In any case he knew that his earlier readings, when susceptible to checking, had been inaccurate. He knew his rough course, but his calculations of position were guesswork.

On 1st November, after 13 days on a south-westerly course, he calculated that he had reached latitude 20 North. He was safely clear of the Sargasso Sea and the doldrums, and he turned due west. He was still optimistic about his rate of progress and believed he would reach the West Indies about 23rd November, after 36 days at sea.[1]

Now, as he steered due west, the fish thinned out significantly and he saw birds only rarely. He still caught enough fish for his needs, but it took him much longer to do it.

A rash which had begun to trouble him early in the voyage had become more general and he was covered with painful little eruptions which greatly aggravated his discomfort in the dinghy. He minimised this as far as possible by sitting on a pneumatic cushion, but suddenly, trying in vain to settle himself comfortably, he knocked it overboard. He did not notice it at first, and then, as the hard wooden floor hurt his skin, he felt for the cushion. Looking round he saw it floating in the distance, perhaps 200 yards away. After

1. In fact he had been drifting almost due south, and though his latitude was correct his longitude was sadly astray. Instead of being 750 miles out into the Atlantic, as he thought, he was little more than 200, still almost in the shadow of the African coastline.

lowering the sail and launching the sea anchor he untied his safety line, stripped off and plunged in after it. He had nearly reached it when, glancing back at the dinghy, he saw to his horror that it was drifting away from him fast.

Something must have fouled the sea anchor. Even without a sail the dinghy, caught in a strong westerly current, was moving too quickly for him to catch it, powerful swimmer though he was.

Once (while training for a cross-Channel attempt) he had swum for 21 hours. In his present debilitated state he knew he could not last for half that time. In desperation he put his last reserves of strength into a fast crawl, lashing at the sea in a frenzy. At first he seemed to gain a little on the dinghy, then he began to slip behind. It was futile to struggle any longer. By an incredible piece of folly he had wrecked the whole experiment and forfeited his life.

He continued to swim mechanically, without hope at first, until he suddenly seemed to be gaining slightly on the dinghy. With a surge of ineffable joy he realised that it had come to a halt. Whatever it was that had fouled the sea anchor, it must somehow have cleared itself.

Only now did he think of the sharks. Most of them were docile, but the occasional one was bad-tempered and belligerent. One of them had already made a deliberate attack on the dinghy. As he pulled himself back on board, physically and morally exhausted, he resolved never to leave the dinghy again.

In addition to his other ills he had now developed a severe inflammation of the salivary gland. When he came to write up his log that night he noticed with a stab of apprehension that his handwriting was deteriorating.

For a week after this incident the trade wind was steady and he made good progress. The patch in the sail held good. There were plenty of fish, and it was no longer necessary to squeeze them to extract the moisture. Two or three cuts and sufficient water would collect. He was never thirsty, but he longed for real fresh water.

The strong wind was accompanied by the occasional squall, in which huge waves broke with destructive violence over the dinghy. After his first swamping Bombard was never quite sure whether the dinghy might founder. If it did, there would be no hope of being picked up. He did not fancy a vain, protracted struggle to keep afloat. He had a supply of barbiturates with him, and he tucked these in his shirt pocket.

On the twenty-fourth day there was a strange, unaccountable calm, the sea glistening like steel under a leaden sky. Then in the distance he heard a roar like a waterfall, the concentrated spattering of millions of droplets on the surface of the sea. Rain! Everything in the dinghy was so salt-encrusted that it was some time before the downpour washed away the residue, but then at last he could drink. There was a slight rubbery impregnation from the tent sheet in which he caught the water, but it was nectar compared with the flavourless, insipid fish-water. He drank his fill, had a luxurious wash, and stored three or four gallons in his rubber mattress after catching it in the tent sheet. Short of some physical calamity, either to himself or the dinghy, he could survive now for several weeks.

But that same afternoon, while he was relaxing and reading a book, there was a sudden and violent blow on the rudder-oar. Thinking it was a shark, against which he believed the rounded surfaces of the dinghy were immune, he looked up unperturbed. What he saw transfixed him with horror. The dinghy was being attacked by a giant swordfish. The rage of the swordfish at the intrusion of this alien craft was plain. Time and again, its dorsal fin bristling, it circled the dinghy before turning in to the attack. Each time, like a boxer who fears the counter-punch, it turned away at the last moment. It must have been on one of these mock attacks that it had collided with the rudder-oar.

It could only be a question of time before the swordfish realised that the dinghy had no defence mechanism. One thrust from that long pointed snout would puncture it irreparably. Two or three such thrusts would destroy it.

As part of his emergency equipment Bombard carried a harpoon (though he had preferred to improvise a weapon for catching fish). There was no doubt that this was an emergency, and he decided to arm himself with it. But he would only use it as a last resort. To attack the swordfish and wound it would only enrage it still further.

With trembling fingers he unlashed the harpoon. But as he turned to face his attacker he dropped it, and it fell into the sea. Through this careless blunder he was reduced to the vulnerability of the true castaway. All he had left was his penknife, converted into the home-made harpoon. He prepared to defend himself with this.

For the rest of the day the swordfish circled the dinghy unceasingly, while Bombard watched with mounting apprehension. Sometimes in its dummy attacks the swordfish would dive straight under the dinghy, bumping against it as it passed underneath, convincing Bombard that the final attack had come. But each time Bombard held his fire, and each time the swordfish flinched from the ultimate encounter. Night fell, and still the swordfish kept up its eternal circuits, interspersed with the occasional feint attack. In the darkness Bombard concentrated on the wake of that ominous dorsal fin. It was not until early morning, after 12 hours of tense anxiety, that the swordfish finally disappeared.

Bombard believed that the swordfish had probably been almost as frightened as he was. This was the only explanation for its failure to attack. It would expect any creature threatened by that thrusting snout to defend itself. Once it had succeeded in drawing fire, once it had taken stock of the enemy defences, Bombard had no doubt it would have moved in for the kill.

From this point on, the long restful nights that he had

enjoyed so far were gone. Every big fish that circled the dinghy after dark looked at first glance like a swordfish. He had to remain watchfully awake.

Next day the birds were so numerous that he believed he must be nearing land, although according to his calculations he would not be there for at least 10 days. He had learned the signs that land was near by heart from the various handbooks he had brought with him on the survival of the castaway. More than half a dozen birds meant that land must be less than 200 miles distant. He had counted at least 10. He did not know that the land to which he was so close was the Cape Verde Islands and that his crossing of the Atlantic had hardly begun. Now came more heavy rain, soaking everything in the dinghy and keeping him in a continual bath of humidity. There were no sharks now, and no swordfish, but he was too wet and miserable to sleep. The one great consolation was that the trade wind was still blowing and that he was making good progress.

By the middle of November he was aware of a serious deterioration in his health. His body and limbs were covered with an angry erupting rash, each spot developing into a hard, wart-like excrescence. The tiniest cut or abrasion quickly turned septic. Yet in spite of all this he remained for the moment optimistic. Although he had lost weight he felt basically strong. He had collected enough water to last a month, and there were still plenty of fish. He still expected to complete the crossing within about a week.

There were still numerous signs—or so he believed—of his proximity to land. The wind blew steadily through the morning, then dropped until mid-afternoon, which was the coastal pattern. And he recognised three distinct types of land bird, none of which was believed to stray more than a hundred miles out to sea. He stayed on watch now day and night, peering for the first glimpse of land.

It was on Sunday, 23rd November, five weeks after leaving the Canaries, that he began to feel uneasy. He could not account for it—it almost seemed that some morbid prescience in the elements themselves had been communicated to him. The sea, which he thought had exhausted its extremes of tranquillity and violence, was brooding and malign, the air at first oppressive and then suddenly chill. He had an inexplicable desire to sail off in another direction, to get as far as possible from the place where he was.

All that day the sense of impending catastrophe continued. The premonition was not vague or amorphous: it was a definite threat, seeming to carry the very aura of death. Even the sunrise was strange, darkened by a thin line of black cloud which spread slowly across the sky during the day like a contagion, turning day into night. Then at last came the storm.

In spite of his forebodings he made up his mind to use the wind to make progress, judging the pressure on the sail carefully, ready to let go before the sail was torn away. For an hour the storm raged, then it dropped as suddenly as it came. As the sail flapped brokenly, he believed he knew the meaning of this orgiastic display of fury. Somewhere not far away there had been a typhoon, or something very like it. Now the elements had exhausted themselves and he was probably faced with a prolonged period of calm.

Day after day the dinghy crawled along, sail inert, drifting imperceptibly towards an unknown destination. Bombard believed that when the storm came he had been less than a hundred miles from land. At his present rate of progress it would take another two or three weeks to get there. But worse than that, he began to have difficulty in maintaining his compass course. He was drifting to the north. If he missed the West Indies he could be many more months at sea.

The truth about Bombard's position was even worse than he imagined. He was still only half-way across the Atlantic. Yet signs of the proximity of land continued to tantalise and deceive him. He caught a fly—that, he thought, must be a sure proof. Then, after a further week of frustrating calm, he caught a butterfly. Land must be incredibly close, and he spent hour after hour straining his eyes in vain for a sight of it.

The baffling absence of any tangible proof that land was near was slowly reducing Bombard to a state of mental anguish that was not far removed from madness. He raved in his log at the wicked deceit of the writer of the castaway's handbook. Everything in the book was a snare and a delusion calculated to drive a sane man out of his mind. He raved at the treacherous trade wind, which had carried him far across the Atlantic only to trap him on the fringe of success. He had rejoiced under an excess of hope. Now, despondent and demoralised, he was sated with despair.

What had he done to Ginette, to their children? What agonies of doubt must she be suffering?

The sun beat down mercilessly, the few clouds that drifted lazily by always seeming to disintegrate before they offered any protection. There was still no wind. He knew that his mind was beginning to fail, and he wondered about his body. Perhaps he was nearer death than he knew.

He had forgotten all about his emergency rations and medical supplies. They did not exist for him, did not come into his calculations at all.

On Saturday, 6th December, after six weeks at sea, he opened his log and began to make his will. As he wrote his hand faltered, then somehow seemed to strengthen. 'I would like to record my last wishes,' he wrote, 'in case I am dead when help arrives.' His uppermost thought was that the notes he had compiled on the voyage should be expanded into a book, the rights to be held by Ginette. He insisted that his thesis about living off the sea had held good, up to a period of 50 days. After that, he conceded, the strain on the human system, mental and physical, became insupportable. But a period of 50 days represented a fantastic advance in scientific and medical knowledge. Most castaways could expect to be seen by a passing ship in that time. His own voyage might fail, but there was no longer any need for castaways to despair.

In his log he went on raving about the maddening and inexcusable errors that found their way into manuals about the sea. In his crazed state he blamed his situation on all kinds of causes. He even began to curse his luck. How could he do otherwise when he saw, or believed he saw, torrents of rain in the distance while above him the sun remained unrelenting?

On 9th December, after a calm lasting for 15 days, the wind blew strongly again, tugging the dinghy gently westwards. The man who lay in the well of the dinghy did not jump up at sunrise next morning to scan the horizon. He had done that too many times, until hope had worn threadbare. He lay with his eyes closed, listless and still. It was mid-morning when he eventually raised himself from the floor of the dinghy and dragged his eyes round the horizon. What he saw made him shout and gesticulate wildly.

'A ship!'

It was the 3,000-ton British cargo steamer *Arakaka*, making for British Guiana, passing right across his bows. Soon the captain was talking to him on the loud hailer.

'Can we help you?'

All he wanted to know was where he was. 'I'd just like a time check, please, and my exact longitude.'

When they gave him his longitude the figures struck him a stunning blow. Instead of being, as he had thought, almost within sight of land, he was still nearly 700 miles out in the Atlantic. Chattering away to himself in confused gibberish, he resolved to give up. Surely 53 days alone at sea without food or water was proof enough.

'Will you come aboard?' asked the captain of the *Arakaka*.

His resistance was gone, he would have to give in. A few

moments later he and the dinghy were hoisted aboard.

'Can we take you on to Georgetown?'

Yes, yes, of course they could. Then something made Bombard hesitate, something from the recesses of memory, the recollection of calumny and ridicule, never to be risked again. He had proved the experts wrong, but they would be all the more anxious to belittle his achievement. 'So you didn't get across the Atlantic after all?' He could hear their sneers. 'You had to accept help, you couldn't make it?' He would die rather than give them the chance to say these things. Somehow, hardly aware of what he was doing, he refused the captain's offer.

An hour later, after a shower and a light meal which the captain insisted he accept, he was back in his dinghy, facing another 700 miles of solitude and privation, unaware whether it might take two weeks or ten, or whether he would ever get there at all. His one great consolation was that Captain Carter had promised to send a message to Ginette. She would at least know that, up to 10th December, he was still alive.

In the next few days Alain Bombard came very near to death. But somehow he completed the rest of the voyage, arriving in Barbados a fortnight later, two days before Christmas. The day after his arrival he received a cable from the captain of the *Arakaka*:

'Congratulations to a gallant gentleman who had so much courage in his convictions to carry on when safety and luxury were proposed. Signed—Carter.'

This message, and the homage of the ordinary sailor and sea-voyager everywhere, did much to sustain him in the many attacks he was to suffer on the integrity and meaning of his voyage, and in the ill-health which afterwards dogged him, caused no doubt by his experiment in the dinghy *L'Hérétique*.

'The shipwrecked do not die of exhaustion,' he wrote later, 'but of despair. An example was needed.' The adventure of Alain Bombard shines as a comfort and inspiration to all those who voyage by sea.

*   *   *

Alain Bombard wrote a full and detailed account of his experiment in *The Bombard Story*, published by André Deutsch in 1953.

5

Ernest Fieldhouse

'It's impossible,' said the colonel. 'You'll never get any more men down there.'

The third-class accommodation of the Japanese transport *Rakoyu Maru* had been stripped of cabins and ablutions and fitted with two rough, tiered platforms on which the Allied prisoners lay. An area that normally held 139 steerage passengers was now crammed with 1,150 British and Australian prisoners of war. There were still another 200 on deck. The Japanese guards kept on pushing them down the stairs, but in that swarming foetid hell-hole below, where the men lay shoulder to shoulder on bare boards, with no ventilation and in total darkness, the point of saturation had been reached. Even the Japanese officers, impatient at first with the colonel's protests, had to admit that he was right.

'All right,' they said, 'we'll leave 200 men on deck. They can change over in rotation, 200 men up and 200 men down, every four hours.' It was a concession of a kind, and the colonel had to accept it.

Gunner Ernest Fieldhouse, 28, small and wiry, with thick, curly black hair, was not untypical of the 1,150 men in the hold. 5 foot 6 inches high, and with a normal weight of $8\frac{1}{2}$ stone, he had gone down to under six stone since his capture by the Japanese. Now, surrounded by a breed of men with whom he shared a single precious quality—an instinct for survival—his small size enabled him to claim, without meeting more than a token hostility, one of the last places in the forward part of the steerage area, closest to the stairway leading up to the deck.

'All men go to Japan,' they had been told. That meant at

least a fortnight at sea. To be near that stairway might mean the difference between life and death.

Men like Ernest Fieldhouse were already survivors—survivors of the Burma-Siam railway, on which they had worked for eighteen months, survivors of the River Kwai, survivors of many months of disease and near-starvation, survivors of periods in which they had seen their comrades die at the rate of 60 a day. Only the fittest of those that remained were being sent to Japan. The remainder would be left to die in Singapore.

Born at Stalybridge, Cheshire in 1916, Fieldhouse had worked in a mill before moving with his parents to the Isle of Man to work with them in the hotel trade. Then, in 1937, at the age of 21, he had joined the Army.

A good student, alert and literate, Fieldhouse had been a member of the St. John's Ambulance Brigade and had always been interested in medicine, so he applied to join the medical corps. He was told that he was not up to the standard physically, and eventually he went into the artillery as a gunner. In 1938 he was posted to Singapore. He had reached the final week of his overseas tour, due to be repatriated, when the Japanese attacked Pearl Harbour.

'All men go to Japan.' Even after the weary months of cruelty and privation, the men were ready to believe in the paradise across the sea that the Japanese guards painted for them. 'All men have new clothes to go with,' was another promise. This amounted to one pair of tight-fitting shorts each. No shirts, no socks, no shoes.

2,000 British and Australian prisoners left River Valley Camp, Singapore on 4th September 1944 on their way to the docks. There they split into two parties. 1,350 of them boarded the Japanese transport *Rakoyu Maru*. The remainder boarded a second transport, the *President Harrison*. Then came the discomfort of being crammed into the bowels of the ship.

At five o'clock that afternoon the two ships pulled out of

the harbour, and two hours later they dropped anchor just outside. There they stayed for the rest of that night and the whole of the next day. Then, at dawn on the morning of 6th September, they sailed for Japan. Ernest Fieldhouse, enjoying the comparative comfort of his four-hour period on deck, watched the land recede.

Within 24 hours the convoy had formed up. Fieldhouse counted 16 ships altogether. There were 9 transports, including tankers, and 7 warships, including an aircraft carrier and several destroyers and frigates. The Japanese clearly meant to get the convoy through.

The gunfire began at midnight, six days out from Singapore. An old field-gun had been mounted in the bows of the *Rakoyu Maru*, and the Japanese fired it at intervals, though to the prisoners on deck there seemed no apparent target. Then, with increasing frequency and violence, the sea began to shudder and erupt with the shock of the depth charges that were being dropped by the destroyer screen. That could mean only one thing—the convoy was under attack by American submarines.

The prisoners below deck still lay in sickly, malodorous darkness, but now they were animated, first listening intently, then chattering among themselves. The men on deck, who were getting a grandstand view of the battle, were shouting the latest news down to their comrades below.

'There goes a tanker!'

The hubbub in the packed steerage accommodation grew to a crescendo as the excitement of the men on deck was conveyed to those below. One by one the ships of the convoy were being sunk. The Yanks were there—perhaps to rescue them.

Three submarines of the American Pacific Fleet, *Growler*, *Pampanito* and *Sealion II*, operating as a pack, had picked up the convoy as it crossed their patrol area, about half-way between Hainan and Luzon, in the South China Sea. The Japanese had detected their presence and had begun to shower the water with depth charges, and the submarines circled warily. Finally, about two hours before dawn, *Growler* blew up a Japanese frigate. In the confusion that followed, the commander of *Sealion II* closed the range.

This was the crucial phase of the Pacific war. Every ship that could be sunk would have its repercussions on some Pacific island, where American troops were fighting to dispossess the Japanese. None of the submarine commanders was aware of the human cargo that two of the transports carried.

At 05.24 the commander of *Sealion II* saw his chance. In the same minute he fired torpedoes at three ships. The first salvo was aimed at a tanker. It found its mark, and the news was shouted down the hatchway to the prisoners below. The second salvo was similarly aimed.

'There goes another tanker!'

Even as the hubbub in the hold of the *Rakoyu Maru* grew to an uproar at this dramatic news, a third salvo was on its way. It had been aimed with no less care and accuracy than its predecessors. It had been aimed at the *Rakoyu Maru*.

The noise that more than 1,100 men can make in a confined space, starved of hope for years, and then suddenly confronted with it, is almost beyond imagining. The clamour and din was deafening. It made the silence when the first torpedo hit the bows of the ship shocking and unbearable. There was a heavy thud forward, the ship shook momentarily, and then the silence below was complete.

'That's *us*.' The voice was no more than a hoarse whisper, but it carried to every man. 'They've hit *us*.'

It was several seconds before the men could accept it, before they could stomach the extinguishing of hope and admit the truth. In those seconds a second torpedo struck the *Rakoyu Maru*, this time hitting the forward hatch, just below where the prisoners lay. The shock of the impact was followed by the sound of rushing wind; soon water began to flow across the steerage area, seeping at first, then spurting and gushing in a great flood.

'Every man for himself.'

The shout came from the prisoners themselves, and a general rush for the stairway began. The darkness was now a nightmare, the narrow escape route for hundreds of men miserably inadequate. Yet the instinct for self-preservation did not quite degenerate into panic. Most of the men reached the deck.

They were too late to get to the boats. There were few enough of them anyway, and already they were filled with Japanese and were being launched by the crew.

The panic on deck was real. Even the Japanese were throwing themselves into the water. Anything that might float was being tossed overboard. Heads were bobbing all round the ship; overloaded rafts were floating, half-submerged; packed lifeboats were drifting, down by the gunwhales. One lifeboat, which had jammed while it was being launched, swung crazily from its davits. The whole scene was lit up by the two blazing tankers. The destroyers were still throwing depth charges, the gun in the bows of the *Rakoyu Maru* was still firing. It was a fantastic scene of chaos and confusion.

Ernest Fieldhouse was one of the first men from the hold to reach the deck, but he was left behind in the rush for lifejackets. Hundreds of them had already been flung overboard, hundreds of men were jumping after them. Fieldhouse himself was too frightened to jump. The ship was still on an even keel, the two Japs on the gun were blazing away, and he decided to stay on board as long as he could.

Loose on the deck, unnoticed by the men who were scrambling for lifejackets, was a square block of rubber, on one side of which was a kind of handle or loop. Fieldhouse grabbed it, gripped it firmly, and held on. He thought it might keep him afloat when the time came.

The scene was now grimly illuminated by the grey light of

dawn. Fieldhouse looked over the side but he was still too scared to jump. Heads were still bobbing about like flotsam, seats, spars and hatch-covers were still being dropped over. Fieldhouse saw one hatch-cover drop right on top of six heads. He looked away. When he looked again the heads were gone.

The gun had stopped firing now. The last stragglers among the crew were disappearing overboard. Fieldhouse suddenly became aware that the ship was almost empty. Yet it was still on an even keel. He didn't think it would sink just yet.

He joined a group of three other men, prisoners like himself. They too had decided they were better off for the moment where they were. One of them, a rough and ready regular soldier, was grinning broadly and throwing out his chest. He had a perverse sense of humour. 'I've been in the Army nearly nine years,' the man was saying. 'I've done C.B., I've been in detention, I've been court-martialled; now I'm the captain of a ship.' Everyone else had gone.

'My stomach's empty,' said Fieldhouse. 'Let's go and see if we can find some grub.'

With the battle still going on around them, the four men went off to find the captain's cabin. On the wall of the cabin was the Japanese flag. On the table were several packets of cigarettes. They were stamped 'Ajax—duty free, for H.M. Ships only.' They now passed back into British hands.

All they could find in the way of food was a sack of soya beans and a sack of sugar. They ate some of the soya beans and chewed some of the sugar. The man with the sense of humour sat himself in the captain's chair. 'Right, you men,' he said. 'Get the ship going. We'd better turn back for Singapore. No, the Japs are there, we'd better make for America. We'll see to the Japs later.' After their years as prisoners it was a dream sequence, the soya beans and the sugar a delicacy, the plentiful supply of cigarettes an impos-

sible luxury. In those few minutes in the captain's cabin of a
sinking ship that everyone else had abandoned they relaxed
and enjoyed themselves, playing a game of make-believe like
children, free men for the first time for three years. They
knew, too, that it would very probably be for the last time as
well.

They were twenty minutes in the captain's cabin before
they decided that they had better face reality again and go
back on deck. The two tankers were still belching thick black
smoke in the distance, the submarines were still being depth-
charged. The *Rakoyu Maru* was listing badly now; it was
time to abandon ship. One by one the four men, still in high
spirits, climbed over the rail and jumped into the sea.

Fieldhouse swam about for some time, holding on to the
square of rubber. Then he saw a great gout of water burst
into the air not more than a hundred yards from him. Half-
stunned, he was lifted bodily out of the water and flung some
distance away from the explosion. He was in the middle of
the battle area and depth-charges were exploding all round
him. He felt numbed and sick, but all his limbs seemed to be
intact. The three men in whose company he had jumped
had disappeared.

Again and again he was lifted out of the water and flung
considerable distances as the depth-charging continued. Yet
he was too numb to feel any pain. Then the blast of a terrific
explosion erupted around him as though from the ocean
bed; this time, completely overwhelmed, he felt himself
being forced down to the depths. But somehow he rose to the
surface, and looking up he saw that the destroyer that had
been throwing the depth-charges had broken in two. One at
least of the submarines had survived the depth-charging and
was still active.

The convoy commander had had enough. Leaving one
destroyer behind to pick up Japanese survivors, he changed
course and headed with all possible speed for Hong Kong.
Any chance that the Americans might pick up the surviving

Allied prisoners disappeared as all three submarines gave chase. Soon the submarine crews, still totally unaware of the plight of the Allied prisoners, were far to the north.

Ernest Fieldhouse was still treading water, hanging on to the square of rubber. He knew he wouldn't be able to hold on like this for long, and he began to swim towards a raft which he saw in the distance. As he approached it he could see that it was hopelessly overloaded. Meant for about 12 it already held at least double that number. The raft itself was partly submerged, so that the men were sitting in two feet of water. Fieldhouse grabbed a rope that was hanging from the side of the raft and hung on.

The soya beans and the sugar had made him unbearably thirsty; they had been unable to find anything to drink on board. He called out to the men on the raft.

'Anyone got anything to drink?'

'There's a chap in the water with a water-bottle round his neck. Why don't you try him?'

Someone pointed the man out, and Fieldhouse swam towards him. 'Give us a drop of water, mate,' he said. Without a word the man unlooped the water-bottle from round his neck and handed it to Fieldhouse. Fieldhouse unscrewed the cap and took a swig. Almost immediately his face contorted and he spat the water out.

'You can't drink this—it's sea-water.'

Only now did Fieldhouse look closely at the man with the water-bottle. He recoiled with horror. The man's eyes were crazed and blood-shot, foam was oozing from his mouth and nostrils. He grabbed viciously at the water-bottle, pushing Fieldhouse under as he did so, and held him there. Fieldhouse struggled wildly, aware that he was in the grip of a madman. Then, as suddenly as the man had turned on him, he relaxed. Fieldhouse broke away and swam back to the raft.

'Let's go back to the ship.'

The *Rakoyu Maru* was still afloat, and several of the men

on the raft thought they might try and reboard her. But even as they were considering it the *Rakoyu Maru* lifted her nose out of the water and slid slowly stern first out of sight.

To Fieldhouse the raft did not look quite so full next morning, and he counted the men on board. There had been 24 last night. Now there were 21. They had lost three men in the night.

Oil from the two tankers was now lying thick on the surface of the sea, and the raft was drifting right through it. Even the men on the raft were getting the lower part of their bodies coated with it. Fieldhouse was soon covered from head to foot.

The water was warm enough in the day-time, but the men shivered throughout the night, when the water seemed to turn ice-cold. After the second night, Fieldhouse counted the men on the raft again. There were 17.

The loss of these men meant that there would be room on the raft for Fieldhouse and perhaps for several others. But Fieldhouse made no move to climb on board. He believed that the men they had lost must have fallen off the raft while they slept. Fieldhouse had not slept at all. He also believed that the thick layer of oil that coated his body was protecting him against death from exposure. It shielded him from the sun during the day, and insulated him from the cold at night.

During the night it began to rain. Fieldhouse, forgetting about the oil, tried to rub the water out of his eyes. All he succeeded in doing was filling them with oil. The oil blinded him; he could not get his eyes clear. Every effort he made to clean them only made them worse. In this situation it was terrifying not to be able to see. As the day wore on he found he was completely blind. He was aware of the difference between light and darkness, and sometimes he could make out a black silhouette on the raft above him, but that was all.

On the morning of the third day there were only four men left on the raft.

All that day Fieldhouse was in a state bordering on delirium. The blinder he became, the more clearly he saw things—palm trees, double-decker buses, lights of many kinds, traffic lights, a fluorescent light that kept flashing on and off, spelling out a sign which he recognised: 'Fish and Chips, Fish and Chips'. In one of these hallucinations he actually smelt the familiar smell, as strong as if he had been passing the shop.

All that day he clung to the rope on the side of the raft, his fingers feeling nothing now, just hanging on by instinct. There was no talking now on the raft, nothing to jerk him out of his delirium. He was in a situation that seemed to have no ending, hour followed hour, night followed day, and he was no longer aware of it. All he knew of past and future was that his name was Fieldhouse and that he was floating alone somewhere in the middle of the Pacific. Rescue did not come into it—he was holding on by instinct until the last moment came.

Rescue, indeed, could not come into it. The destroyer had stayed to pick up Japanese survivors, but it had ignored the Allied prisoners. Then it had raced after the convoy. The three submarines, too, had chased the convoy towards Hong Kong. There were no ships within hundreds of miles, and no aircraft either.

When dawn came on the morning of 15th September, Fieldhouse was aware of nothing except that his fingers were still curled round the rope of the raft and that he was safe for the moment. He shouted to the men on the raft, but there was no answer. The raft must be empty. He was alone.

He reached up to grip the surface of the raft, but he could feel nothing. Nothing. He grabbed with both hands at the rope, but he could not feel it or sense it. Slowly the truth dawned on him that there was no rope, and no raft either. The fingers that he had thought were locked round the rope were still clenched, but they were gripping nothing. In his delirium during the night he had lost contact with the raft and drifted away from it.

In a moment of panic he struck out, but he quickly realised the stupidity of it. He shouted again, but no answer came. In his blinded state he would never regain the raft.

He was treading water mechanically, his body surprisingly buoyant. How long he went on like that, how long he had been treading water already, he did not know. But during the day he brushed against something in the water. It was a body. Whether it was Japanese or British he did not know, but the man was floating just below the surface, certainly dead. He felt excitedly round the man's body. Yes—he had a lifejacket on.

Turning the body over in the water, feeling for the straps that he could not see, untying them, tugging the jacket free—all this took him an interminable time. Yet he worked methodically. When knots and straps seemed impossible to unravel he tried to keep calm. To help him in his labours, the body itself acted as a sort of raft, holding him up.

At last he had the lifejacket free and over his shoulders. He was still 200 miles from land, and had he been able to see he would have known that there was not a ship in sight, yet he felt ridiculously safe. For the first time for many hours he relaxed.

Soon he was delirious again, protected from reality by delusions. He could hear the noise of motor traffic now, and presently it seemed that some huge monster shape, perhaps a whale, was rising in front of him out of the sea. Yet he felt no fear. The whirring of engines filled his ears, the monster shape towered above him, a black shadow between him and the sun.

Someone was shouting at him. 'Who are you?' the voice seemed to say. 'Who are you?' He could not answer, dumb and paralysed as in a dream. But was it a dream? Or was there really a voice calling to him, incredibly near?

'British and Australian.' That was the answer to the question he had been asked, and somehow he croaked the words out. 'British and Australian.' After many hours alone, his answer showed that he still retained a sense of comradeship with his fellow prisoners.

Rescue had indeed come, a rescue that was hardly less than a miracle, yet when it seemed that strong arms were grabbing him, and that someone was trying to pass a rope round his waist, Fieldhouse remembered the madman with the water-bottle, and he struggled with what strength he still had. 'Take it easy,' said the voice. 'Relax, bud.'

The submarine *Pampanito* had hung on to the Jap convoy for two days, sinking another tanker and a big transport, the 10,509 ton *Kachidoki Maru*. The commander had then headed back for his patrol area. In doing so he had passed right through the waters in which he had made his initial attack on the convoy. During the day he had surfaced within a hundred yards of Fieldhouse. Even then the crew thought they might not have seen him but for his black, curly hair.

Commander Summers of the *Pampanito* then began a systematic search of the area. Soon he found a number of rafts loaded with men. Many were dead, others were dying. Of the 1,350 prisoners who had sailed on the *Rakoyu Maru*, only about 200 were still alive.

Summers knew that the *Sealion II* was also in the area, and he called on her commander for help. By eight o'clock that night there were 71 emaciated, oil-covered men on *Pampanito* and another 50 on *Sealion II*, 121 men altogether. It was all the two submarines could take and still leave a margin for safety.

Meanwhile Summers had radioed to two more submarines, *Barb* and *Queenfish*, for further assistance. 'It was heartbreaking', wrote Summers in his log, 'to leave so many dying men behind.' 30 more men were rescued later by the second two submarines, but 7 of them died before the submarines reached port. Fieldhouse himself was unconscious on board *Pampanito* for more than two days.

The survivors were taken to Saipan and thence to Honolulu, then across America and home aboard the *Queen Mary*. Back in England, Fieldhouse was told that he had been knocked about too much to stay in the artillery. He was given a choice of two units—the Pay Corps, and, ironically, the Medical Corps. The workings of the British Army were unfathomable: without reproach or comment, he transferred to the Medical Corps, the service of his original choice.

* * *

In the post-war years Ernest Fieldhouse has twice suffered the collapse of both lungs. He has had a coronary thrombosis, also a stomach ulcer. But each time, with a buoyancy reminiscent of the 84 hours in which he stayed afloat in the Pacific, he has somehow bounced back to the surface. This man with the resilience of india-rubber has never drawn a disability pension; and on his 53rd birthday on Boxing Day 1969 he described himself as 'fighting fit'. Since then he has sustained severe muscular injuries and sprains in a fall at work, but after a period of hobbling about on a stick he is almost back to normal.

6

The Sands of Dee

On the promenade at Rhyl, by the clock tower to the left of
the pier, an attractive, bright-faced woman, whose greying
hair is beginning to betray her middle age, is rattling a collecting box and offering a familiar emblem to the crowds of
holidaymakers as they jostle by. On the other side of the
clock tower her husband, a relaxed, imperturbable Man-
cunian, has another box and is doing his best to compete
with the candy-floss and ice-cream vendors and the hubbub
of the amusement arcades. Elsewhere on the promenade two
more collectors, both fair-haired young men, are conducting
a brisk trade with their boxes despite frequent interruptions
from people who seem to know them well. A third member
of the family, a daughter Pat, is also collecting amongst the
crowd.

This is the Mullins family, and they are on their annual
pilgrimage to Rhyl. They have been going back there every
year for 20 years. They are not on holiday—they are day
trippers who left home at seven o'clock in the morning to
catch the early crowds on the promenade. At lunch-time
they will open their picnic baskets and stop briefly for re-
freshment before getting back to the job. Over the years, in
their home town of Sale and at Rhyl on Lifeboat Day, they
have collected hundreds of pounds for the cause.

It is a warm summer breeze that blows along the North
Wales coastline; not the bitter wind of man's ingratitude.
The Mullins family have a debt that they know they can
never repay. But neither will they ever forget. For it was
along this coast in August 1950 that stark tragedy suddenly
faced them, literally out of a clear blue sky.

Eight miles along the coast east of Rhyl, past Prestatyn and along the sand dunes to the Dee estuary, stands the Point of Air lighthouse, an old, disused lighthouse that has been privately owned for the whole of this century. Standing at the top of the beach, it commands a magnificent view of the river mouth, and of West Kirby and Hoylake on the Wirral peninsula, five miles away on the far side of the Dee. (Beyond this peninsula lies the Mersey.) Otherwise the beach is utterly bare, not a building or habitation in sight. Behind the lighthouse lie the sand-dunes, stretching inland for several hundred yards, and then comes the straggling holiday settlement of Talacre, a mixture of small neat bungalows and dilapidated shanties. It was in one of these bungalows that the Mullins family spent August Bank Holiday week in that far-off summer of 1950.

Talacre is an ideal holiday spot for youngsters, and this was the main reason why John Mullins, a 35-year-old sales executive with an engineering firm, had chosen it. With three young children life was a bit of a struggle, and renting the bungalow meant a comparatively cheap holiday. It was not too far from home, either, and the whole family travelled down from Sale on the motor-cycle combination which was the only transport Mullins could afford to run in those days. Dorothy Mullins sat in the side-car with her younger son John, six years old, and her 18-month-old daughter Pat. The ten-year-old David rode pillion behind his father. Strapped to the top of the combination was their luggage, and on top of that was a deflated rubber dinghy, ex-R.A.F. stores, bomber type, big enough to take six men comfortably and several more in emergency.

Mullins had bought the dinghy as a sort of garden pool for the boys to play in; he had not intended to take it to Talacre. Dinghies, he knew, could be dangerous; they were difficult to control and were easily carried out to sea. But David and John persuaded him. 'We won't take it far out, honest, Dad.' 'Honest, Dad, we'll do whatever you say.' And he had relented.

Wednesday 9th August was calm and sunny, and after breakfast the two boys inflated the dinghy, helped by their father. Even with the aid of a pump it took them most of the morning, and it was after lunch before they took it down to the beach.

'Can we take it out now, Dad?'

Attached to the dinghy was a lifeline about 100 feet long, with a rubber ring at the end of it. The tide was right out, and after dragging the dinghy for some distance until they reached the shallows, John Mullins took a stout beach spade, dug a hole some two feet deep in the wet sand, threaded the spade through the rubber ring, and buried it. Now the dinghy was firmly anchored to the beach. The whole family—John and the boys, and Dorothy with the baby in her arms—then waded into the sea and got in the dinghy. Apart from shoes and socks they were fully clothed.

In the excitement of launching the dinghy none of the family had noticed that the sky had clouded over. Although they were only a few yards out the sea was becoming choppy, and several times a wave hit the rim of the dinghy and splashed over the top. For the boys it was fun, but soon Dorothy Mullins climbed out of the dinghy with her baby and waded ashore.

The dinghy was now being pushed out to sea by an off-shore wind, and soon the lifeline connecting them to the beach pulled taut. The anchorage was strong enough to hold for a time. But the combined weight of the dinghy and its occupants, coupled with the force of the wind, slowly loosened the anchorage. Looking shorewards they suddenly realised they were drifting out to sea.

The lighthouse seemed incredibly distant—but this no doubt was because the tide was so far out. They were still in shallow water. There could be no real problem. All John Mullins had to do was get out of the dinghy, grab the lifeline and tow the boys in. He couldn't actually see the bottom as he climbed over the rim, but he knew it must be there.

In fact, unknown to John Mullins, the sandy bottom was a switchback of gutters and gullies all the way down from Rhyl. It was into one of these gullies, some of them the width of a racecourse, that he now disappeared. Feeling in vain for the bottom, he struck out and regained the surface. Working back to the dinghy, he grasped the lifeline and began swimming shorewards, towing the dinghy behind him.

Mullins was not a strong swimmer, and from sea-level the shore was beginning to look more and more remote. He tried the breast-stroke, he tried swimming on his side, then turned over on his back to rest, but very quickly he realised that towing the dinghy against the stiffening off-shore wind was beyond his strength. He would need help, and he began to shout for it.

Looking round he saw two other swimmers who he judged were within earshot. 'Help! Get hold of this rope with me!'

One swimmer came quite close to him, but he stared at Mullins in alarm. There was no mistaking his reaction—don't get involved or you may be dragged down yourself. To Mullins' despair this swimmer turned away. Perhaps he too had been caught by the wind and was struggling to get back.

Mullins looked round at the dinghy. Both the boys were standing up, watching him, and he was terrified that they might capsize the dinghy or fall overboard. Neither of them could swim. 'Sit down!' he called. 'Don't move. I'll go and get help.'

Sitting on the beach, Dorothy Mullins heard her husband's cries for help and looked round to see if she could enlist anyone's aid. There were not more than a dozen people on their part of the beach and no one seemed able to help. She put her baby down on the sand, and as she did so she saw a woman walking along the beach. 'Keep an eye on my baby for me,' she called, and then she ran seawards.

Splashing through the shallows, she soon reached the deep

water and struck out towards her husband. She too was a poor swimmer, but she reached him and gave him what help she could. By this time he was nearly exhausted, breathing badly and swallowing water, and within a minute or so she was nearly as distressed herself. They were still only half-way across the deep gully and they were making no progress at all. They were almost beaten, coughing and gulping, when another holidaymaker, Mr. W. Chrimes, of Altrincham, the neighbouring town to Sale, saw their plight. With the help of his son and a friend he was just in time to save them, and a minute or two later they were prostrate on the beach, sick with shock and the sea-water they had swallowed.

Within a few seconds both staggered to their feet and began to go back to the water. The dinghy was becoming difficult to pick out, visible only intermittently as it rose and fell in the choppy sea. In a frenzy of terror for her children, Dorothy Mullins began to run forward, determined to swim out to the dinghy. Her husband was too weak to stop her, but Chrimes intervened. As he stood in front of her she beat her fists against his chest in anger and frustration, but he over-powered her and eventually calmed her down. 'My son's gone to get help,' he told her. 'They'll get a boat out to them as soon as possible. These dinghies are unsinkable. They'll be perfectly all right.'

Gerald, the Chrimes' 16-year-old son, was already on his way to the Talacre shops to phone the police. Stumbling across the sand dunes, he raced along the unmade track for a mile or more to the first of the little grocery shops that had a telephone. There he dialled 999. His call was answered by the police at Prestatyn, four miles away. 'We'll have some-one along there at once,' they told him. The time was ten minutes past four and it was already half an hour since the dinghy had drifted out to sea. From the beach it was no longer visible.

At 4.12 the telephone rang in the Coastguard office at Rhyl. 'Prestatyn Police here. We've just had a message that a rubber dinghy with two children in it is drifting out to sea off the Point of Air Lighthouse.' The coastguard at Rhyl rang the Rhyl lifeboat secretary, and at 4.15 the maroons were fired to call out the lifeboat crew.

The R.A.F. had no helicopter rescue service in August 1950. There were no inshore rescue boats. It was the lifeboat service or nothing.

Fifteen minutes later the lifeboat was clear of the boat-house and an amphibious tractor was towing it down the beach to the sea. Soon the tractor was in water deep enough for launching. But there was no sign of the coxswain. He was in a marquee at the far end of the town and had not heard the maroons. The second coxswain, Billy Hunt, who had not been out before on a service as first coxswain, took charge.

All but one of the seven-man crew were volunteers who had been called from their normal occupations by the maroons. Nearly all had been professional seamen at some time in their lives. The task of motoring along the coast to the Point of Air Lighthouse looked simple enough, but there were complications. The corrugations along this coastline were so severe, and the sandbanks at low tide lay so far out, that only skilful navigation from local knowledge would get them through the shoals without running aground. To make matters more difficult, the corrugations varied with the time of year and with wind, tide and weather, so that only daily observation could keep a coxswain abreast of the changes.

Another problem would be that the biggest sandbanks of all were down the coast off the Point of Air and beyond. First there was the West Hoyle Bank, running parallel with the coast about three miles out all the way from Prestatyn, blocking the entrance to the Dee. Beyond that the East Hoyle Bank cut the Wirral peninsula off altogether at low water, ruling out help from that side. Then there was the mouth of the Dee itself, a vast expanse of sand and marsh at low tide.

The Hoyle banks, however, might act as a barrier, at least

for a time, and they ought to find the dinghy somewhere in the Dee estuary. The tide had been on the flood for less than two hours and still had four hours to run, which was just as well. Towards high tide the banks and mud flats would be completely covered, and then the tidal flood, baulked by the outfall from the river, boiled over the shallows like a cauldron, flinging up a wall of spray that could be seen in the glasses from Rhyl.

Even with the help of all their local knowledge it would take at least an hour to sneak along through the shallows past Prestatyn to the lighthouse. But by that time, perhaps, they would have some news of where the boys were. It would still want about three hours to high tide.

Five minutes after launching, Hunt received a message on his voice radio. 'The latest information is that the dinghy when last seen appeared to be drifting towards Mostyn.' Mostyn was a tiny port just inside the mouth of the Dee; if the tide had driven the dinghy into the estuary it would be much easier to find. It had sounded at first as though the dinghy might be driven out to sea.

Lying flat in the bottom of the dinghy, David and John Mullins were feeling nothing more as yet than a slight chill of uneasiness that was not altogether unpleasurable. To them the dinghy seemed huge, the rim as tall as the sides of a boat. Occasionally they sat up far enough to peer over the rim, and the first time they did so they saw their mother apparently waving to them; in fact she was motioning to them to lie down. The next time they ventured to sit up, the few scattered figures on the beach were no longer recognisable. Soon even the beach itself disappeared.

When John began to whimper, David reassured him. 'We'll drift to an island, where there'll be houses. Then we'll 'phone them to come for us.' He believed that this would happen. But next time he sat up there was nothing in sight but sea. Then, just ahead of him, he spotted a floating buoy.

If he could grap that buoy and hold on, that would stop them drifting further. But he could see that he wouldn't be able to reach it. Then he remembered the lifeline. If he could somehow coil that round the buoy it would hold them. He pulled the lifeline in, swung it above his head like a lasso, and flung it across the intervening water. The rubber ring hit the buoy but bounced off. He tried again.

The second time, thrown off his balance by the roughening sea, he missed the buoy altogether. But the third time his aim was accurate and the line fell exactly right, wrapping itself tightly round the buoy. The dinghy drifted on, and then the rope pulled taut. For a moment it held. Then, dragged by the drifting dinghy, the rope slipped on the smooth surface of the buoy and loosened. Soon they were out of range of the buoy, once again heading out to sea.

The wind was taking them in a north-easterly direction, and the buoy they had passed marked the limit of the safe channel for shipping rounding the Point of Air Lighthouse heading for Mostyn. Beyond it the depth of the water decreased rapidly. Soon, looking over the side, David noticed with astonishment that he could see the bottom.

It seemed impossible. They were much too far out to sea. Yet there was no doubt about it. The water was only two or three feet deep. They must be coming to an island. He climbed out of the dinghy and dropped down into the water, and then, straight ahead, he saw a stretch of sand. 'Look, John,' he called, 'a desert island. Come and help me pull the dinghy there.' And John got out and joined him in the water.

They dragged the dinghy behind them until they reached the island, then hauled it ashore, pulling it right up to the highest point. Then they dug into the sand with their hands, as they had seen their father do, and buried the lifeline. They were right in the centre of the island, and they felt much safer. But there was no sign of the promised houses. The clouds had darkened, a rolling mist lay over the estuary, and a gusting wind was sweeping fiercely across the island, blowing loose sand with it, stinging their legs painfully. Then they heard a staccato pattering from inside the dinghy. It had begun to rain.

'We'll get under the dinghy,' said David. 'That'll shelter us.' He had seen his father turn it upside down in the garden so that they could use it as a tent, and he began to lift it from one side. 'Give us a hand to turn it over, John.'

As soon as they began to lift the dinghy, the wind caught it like a sail. Struggling to turn it upside down, they felt the overwhelming force of the wind as it wrenched the dinghy from their grasp. Vertical, running on its rim like a wheel, the dinghy ripped its line out of the sand and cavorted across the island, the two boys racing after it. Travelling at incredible speed, it spun away like a hoop, off the island and across the water until it disappeared from sight. They had lost their only protection against wind and sea.

'Surely this island's getting smaller?'

David was beginning to realise that it wasn't an island at all. The sand which had seemed a few minutes ago to stretch an infinite distance had now assumed a definite shape, bounded on all sides by sea. And the sea was encroaching still further each minute.

'They're bound to send a boat,' said David, keeping up their spirits. 'They're bound to be here soon.'

The Rhyl lifeboat was making good time along the coast, following the line of marker buoys inshore and making use of the known gutters and gullies. Hunt was at the wheel, Hughes, the mechanic, was at the engine controls, and everyone else was on look-out. An hour after leaving Rhyl they passed the Point of Air lighthouse and headed for the Dee flats. Their last message had told them that the dinghy was drifting towards Mostyn, so they began to search up-river. Within a minute or so they spotted the Mostyn pilot-boat, which had also been called out by the coastguard, and they hailed it at once. The little pilot-boat had combed the river-mouth, but it could not cope with the broken waters of the estuary. 'We've sighted nothing in this part of the river,' said the pilot. 'They must have drifted out towards the Hoyle banks.'

The lifeboat turned down-river and headed out to sea. The time was nearly six o'clock and the tide was making fast.

On the sandbank, David and John huddled together for warmth and support as the water rose. First they moved back as it approached them, only to find that it was closing in just as quickly behind them. Soon it was rippling over their feet, then it covered their ankles. It was not long before it was up to John's waist. There came a time when David had to grab John or he would have gone under. He held him at first in his arms but then, as the water deepened, he could no longer keep him clear of the waves as the current slopped and eddied around him, and he hoisted him up on his shoulders. By that time the sea was up to his armpits, and as the tidal flood surged past him he had to keep moving about on the same spot all the time to retain a foothold. Then his feet began sinking into the sand.

'I'll have to let you go in a minute, John. I'm going under.'

He knew he was at the highest point of the sandbank and that it was no good moving elsewhere. Two or three minutes, perhaps, and the water would wash over his head.

Steering unerringly through the Dee flats, bumping oc-casionally on the sandy bottom but avoiding the worst of the shallows, Coxswain Hunt, having studied the wind direction in the estuary and taken bearings on the lighthouse, had estimated that the dinghy must have drifted to the eastern extremity of the West Hoyle bank. He doubted if they could get through the shoals yet, but it was worth a try. The sea on the edge of the bank was already frothing with spume and if they didn't find the boys soon it might be too late.

One of the crewmen, George Povah, scanning the bank through binoculars, shouted that he thought he could see something. 'Hold her steady, Billy!' The lurch of the lifeboat on the swell made it impossible to keep his gaze riveted, but eventually he focused on what he was looking for.

'It's like two footballs,' he shouted. 'It could be the boys' heads.'

They were almost on course for the two blobs Povah had sighted, and they steered at once towards them. Hunt altered his helm this way and that, while one man took soundings with a weighted line and another kept plunging a boathook into the water and calling out the depth. But the corrugations here were shifting and unpredictable. They had got to within 200 yards of the boys when they grounded on a hidden sandbank.

'Get a rocket line ready,' shouted Hunt.

They could see the boys quite clearly now, struggling to keep their heads above water in the rapidly rising tide. That tide would refloat the lifeboat within minutes, but by then it would have drowned the boys. A rocket line was the quickest way of reaching them, but the boys would have no means of securing it.

'Two volunteers to go and get them,' shouted Hunt.

George Povah and another crewman, Jack Alcock, sprang over the side and began wading through the water. 'Wait!' shouted Hunt. 'Take a line with you.' Neither man could swim, and although both were wearing lifejackets Hunt knew there were deep gullies and powerful currents between them and the boys. Quickly each man tied on to a line, and then they set out.

'Don't move,' shouted Hunt to the boys through a mega-phone. 'You're surrounded by treacherous gullies. We're coming to get you.'

The increasing depth of the water was already threat-ening to choke David. It was up to his neck, and the dis-turbed surface was flooding over his head every few seconds and he was gulping water as he fought for breath. His legs were leaden, he could hardly feel the bottom, and once or twice he was swept off his feet. From sea level he could see nothing of the lifeboat for most of the time, or of the men who were coming to get them, and only the desperate urgings of his brother, who could see that rescue was im-inent, sustained him in that last half-minute. Then strong arms lifted both boys up, and they were carried back to the lifeboat.

It was 6.17, two hours after they had been called out, when Hunt sent a final signal on his voice radio. 'Have picked up both children. Am aground on East Hoyle bank but am O.K. Am trying to get off, and will then proceed to Rhyl. Please have an ambulance and a doctor waiting.'

The boys were so far from the lighthouse that their parents did not see the rescue although they were peering through binoculars from the top of the lighthouse the whole time. It was not until the lifeboat returned on its way back to Rhyl and Hunt called out to the shore through a megaphone as he passed the lighthouse that they knew their children were safe. Then they were driven by the police into Rhyl.

A huge holiday crowd cheered rescuers and rescued when they reached the boathouse at 8 o'clock that evening. The tide by then was full.

It was not until Dorothy Mullins saw for herself that her boys were all right that she remembered she had left her baby with a perfect stranger on the beach at Talacre five hours earlier. After such an ordeal, this rare lapse of memory can perhaps be understood and forgiven. Forgetting is not normally a Mullins trait.

7

Carlsen and the Flying Enterprise

The saloon of the 6,700-ton merchantman *Flying Enterprise* was gay with paper-chains and coloured fairy lights. Yet it was empty. In preparing the turkey and Christmas pudding the negro cook had excelled himself. Yet none of the ten passengers—five women, an 11-year-old boy, and four men—felt like eating their Christmas dinner.

Ever since sailing from Hamburg on 21st December bound for New York (the year was 1951) the weather had been bad. First it had been fog, hampering them as they crept down the Elbe, slowing them to a crawl as they traversed the North Sea and English Channel. Then had come the gale warnings. On Christmas morning the sea had roughened and the wave-crests had been streaked with foam. The air had been charged with flying spume and spindrift and rain squalls had swept the deck. And during the night, as they approached the open Atlantic, they began to hit the vortex of the storm.

Towards morning the *Flying Enterprise* was being pounded and battered in mountainous seas and the wind had reached hurricane force. Blocks of ocean as big as icebergs were colliding with the hull with torpedo force, blasting the seasick passengers out of their bunks and hurling them from one side of their cabins to the other. Lightning flashed with terrifying suddenness in the heavens, like a blown fuse, while the shrill caterwauling of the elements drowned even the explosions of thunder which followed. They were caught in the middle of a vast cauldron of water, a violent convulsion of wind and sea.

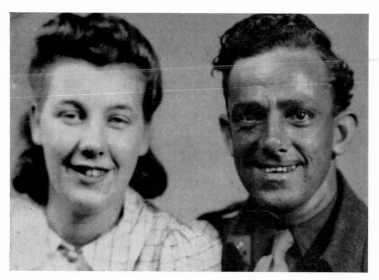

5a   Ernest and Dorothy Fieldhouse

5b   John and David Mullins in the lifeboat after rescue

6 The listing *Flying Enterprise*: Carlsen and Dancy can be seen outside the starboard rail near the stern. (Inset) Captain Kurt Carlsen

All over the eastern Atlantic, ships were giving out distress signals. The *Queen Mary,* three days late, was battling through its worst crossing ever. Most of the bridge of a Norwegian freighter was swept away, and the captain and first officer with it. A Dutch coaster, its lifeboats torn asunder, was driven aground near Biarritz and all its crew lost. A large Norwegian tanker buckled and broke in two 50 miles off Corunna. Even ships sheltering in harbour dragged their anchors and collided with each other. In San Sebastian, 200 people were injured when a 75-mile-an-hour gale swept the town. It was the worst Atlantic storm for 37 years.

Captain Kurt Carlsen, master of the *Flying Enterprise,* called to the engine-room to slow down. Some of his cargo was uncrated, and if it loosened it might be damaged. His passengers, too, would suffer less if the ship were hove to. Soon the propellers were idling, turning just enough to maintain steerageway and keep the ship heading off wind. Now she would ride out the storm.

The 37-year-old Carlsen, a short, stocky Dane who had become a naturalised American during the war, was no ordinary seaman. His face, still youthful and fresh complexioned, was unmistakably Scandinavian and seafaring. For him, a married man with two young children, it had been a lonely Christmas. But as a master he was accustomed to solitude.

Kurt Carlsen was not the sociable, easily approachable type of sea-captain. He believed in keeping his men at a distance. It was fatal to make friends on board, even among one's most trusted officers. It was bad for discipline. He preferred the kind of love-hate relationship which had existed between him and his own favourite commanders. Half the time the crew might long to knife him, but that was how they liked to feel about their man. That jutting nose that almost overlapped the upper lip when he smiled, that rectangular jaw, were the symbols of a man apart.

All Christmas night the storm raged with unabated fury,

H

and with the coming of daylight the clashing elements seemed to unite at last in a single paroxysm of destructive energy. It was at seven o'clock on Boxing morning, with the hurricane at its height, that an ear-splitting detonation from somewhere forward of the square white superstructure convinced all on board that the ship had struck a rock or a mine.

'All hands on deck!'

The damage did not take long to find. The vessel had cracked amidships in two places, from starboard to port, across the deck and down the plated hull, opening up a $\frac{1}{2}$-inch fissure above and around the No. 3 hold. Feverishly a repair gang worked on the damage, lashing the cable-posts together on either side of the gap, filling the crack with concrete. The incident was not altogether outside Carlsen's experience, but he reported it at once to the owners by radio, postponing a decision on what port he would make for until the storm subsided.

All that day, Boxing Day, the passengers stayed in their cabins, refusing food, unaware that the ship was letting in water almost as fast as the crew could pump it out. It was not until early next morning that the wind eased and Carlsen felt able to get under way again. In the hurricane the ship had drifted north, and Carlsen wanted to get down into the shipping lanes in case he should need help.

Working as well as they could in the waterlogged engine-room, the engineers and firemen managed to keep the ship steaming at around ten knots. But the winds were still fierce and the seas mountainous. And building up to the south-west, gathering its strength for another murderous assault, was a second cyclonic storm.

It hit the ship at half-past eleven that morning. First the hull seemed to be thrust up out of the water by a hidden hand, teed up, like a golf ball. Then with a mighty swing the ocean fell upon the *Flying Enterprise*, driving her sideways and down, burying her in thousands of tons of water, knocking her off her course. As the ship's natural buoyancy brought her up again after the knock-down, another lethal broadside pinned her over as in a wrestling match, bending her shoulders to the sea. The starboard lifeboat was smashed in like a match-box, furniture was prised loose from the steel bulkheads to which it was riveted, the compasses were shot from their binnacles, the cross-trees on the foremast dipped into the water, the ship was overwhelmed by a flying flood of sea. Water poured through the cracks in the hull and seeped through the broken deck. No. 3 Hold was flooded and a tidal-wave swept through the engine-room. When at last the sea retreated, as though to survey its handiwork, the *Flying Enterprise* lay twisted and broken, stooped under the weight of its injuries, slowing to a halt and listing drunkenly to port.

Within a few minutes, in spite of the frantic efforts of the men at the pumps, the ship slumped into a steeper list as her cargo shifted a second time, settling at an angle of 30 degrees to the water.

'Full speed ahead!'

Carlsen was trying to right the ship by applying the wheel hard a-starboard under full power. But the turbines, deprived of oil by the heavy list, would not respond.

'Get the passengers out of their cabins. Assemble them in the passageways on the cabin deck.'

Carlsen believed that the ship would float and that there was no immediate danger of capsizing, but he was taking no chances. He called his radio room. 'Send an emergency signal.' There was no shipping within several hours' steaming of them, but within three minutes the American freighter *Southland* had acknowledged their signal and changed course to assist them. The time was precisely one o'clock on the afternoon of Friday 28th December and they were some 400 miles south-west of Land's End. Twenty minutes later there was another great earthquake lurch on board the *Flying Enterprise* as she keeled over still further to port, finally settling at an angle of 45 degrees. Deck and walls now sloped at the same angle, making progress about the ship difficult and hazardous. Heavy seas still swamped the deck, and the rail on the port side was awash. There was no hope now of restarting the engines.

Carlsen called his wireless operator again. 'Send out an S.O.S. Say that we need all the assistance we can get. But keep it short to save the batteries. They may have to last a long time.'

It was not until after dark that the *Southland* made visual contact with the *Flying Enterprise*. The passengers, cold and hungry, many still in their night-clothes, huddled together in the jamb of the passage-way, soaked by the heavy seas which still washed around the superstructure and flooded the darkened corridors. They were greatly encouraged when they saw the freighter's lights. The *Southland* stood by all night, ready to attempt a rescue operation next morning.

At dawn the lifeboat was ready and a crew standing by. The seas were still mountainous, and a Norwegian tanker that had appeared on the scene pumped out hundreds of tons of oil in an attempt to subdue them. Then the rescue work began. The passengers were taken up to the port rail on the bridge deck, high in the sloping superstructure, and from there they were urged to jump into the water, to be picked up by the lifeboat. The seas were lashing angrily below them, and one by one they hesitated.

Several members of the crew, on orders from Carlsen, showed the way by grabbing a line and jumping into the sea, to be picked up by the lifeboat. Carlsen stood by the rail with his passengers.

'Are you ready to go now?'

The nearest person to him was a German woman named Frau Muller. She was the mother of the 11-year-old boy Lothar. Her 19-year-old daughter Liane was also with her. Someone had to go first. As a mother Frau Muller had to set the example to her children. She jumped. She clutched the line but lost it as the swell cut her off from the lifeboat. Liane wanted to keep with her mother and she jumped after her. It was twenty minutes before they were picked up. Lothar, too frightened to jump, stayed on the ship.

None of the other passengers was willing to jump into that icy, rolling, tempestuous sea. The lifeboat crew shouted at them by loud hailer, telling them to climb round to the stern, where they could step off more easily into the water, but still they clung uncertainly to the rail. It was Carlsen who re-solved the impasse. He gave orders to his crew. 'Each man is to take a passenger and jump with them. Jump together and hang on to them.'

The negro cook took Lothar Muller by the shoulders. 'How's about it, sonny? Shall we go?'

Lothar nodded, and the cook embraced him tightly and jumped. Soon they were both aboard the lifeboat. Each pas-senger then jumped with a member of the crew. One woman, separated from her escort by a 40-foot wave, was carried far beyond the lifeboat. Half an hour later she was hauled out, unconscious and black with oil. She recovered aboard the *Southland*.

Several other ships had now reached the rescue scene and were putting down boats. But the weather was deteriorating, making the work of rescue more and more difficult. One lifeboat, from the American military transport *General Greeley*, crashed into the *Southland*'s boat as the two were manoeuvring alongside, putting both boats out of action. A launch put down by the tanker was also in trouble. The engine stalled, the rudder smashed against the tanker's side, and the nine-man rescue party scrambled back on board as the launch was swept away.

Several crewmen missed the lifeboats and drifted help-lessly away out of sight. But of all these men only one, a stateless seaman named Bunjakowski, was drowned. With him was his pet dog.

A volunteer party made ready to stay on board, but as the ship settled deeper and listed more acutely Carlsen would not let them stay. 'Get off the ship,' he told them. 'That's an order.' So by nightfall all the passengers and crew had gone—all, that is, except the master, Kurt Carlsen. He resolutely refused to go. As the last lifeboat left the ship he stood at the top of the sloping bridge deck, hand on rail to steady himself, waving farewell.

Carlsen's decision to stay on board was not taken wholly out of sentiment. The hull was fractured and waterlogged, but the ship had found a new gravity centre, and if the superstructure held there was a chance that she might float for some time. As long as he was on board he could assess the chances of a salvage operation. If a fast tug could be got pretty soon, there was still a chance that the ship, together with her valuable cargo, could be towed into port.

Under marine law governing salvage, Carlsen was protecting the owners by sticking to his ship. That was a part of his duty to them, and to the insurers. By staying on board he might make just the difference between failure and success. But when all these things had been carefully weighed there remained one compelling reason why Kurt Carlsen stayed on board, precariously perched, prepared at any moment to be shot into the sea, or to be sucked under by a capsizing ship. It was not a matter of obligation or duty, and it had nothing to do with dollars. He had been at sea since he was 15. He had been a master for four years. He knew the sea's traditions, understood and cherished the mystique. As long as his ship stayed afloat he would not leave her.

But because of the terrible weather about 15 ships in the Western Approaches were urgently in need of assistance, and nearly every available tug was already engaged. In any case the *Flying Enterprise* was apparently sinking, and towing doomed ships didn't pay. Of the bigger tugs, the *Turmoil* was towing a Shell tanker to Falmouth, and the Dutch tug *Zwarte Zee* was towing another British ship. Only the *Zwarte Zee*'s sister ship, the *Oceaan* was available, and the freighter's owners quickly engaged her. The heartening news was relayed at once to Carlsen—but next morning came bitter disappointment. The *Oceaan* was only a short distance from the *Flying Enterprise* when she got news by radio that the *Zwarte Zee* had collided with another vessel and had had to slip her tow to save herself; the *Oceaan*, not unnaturally, went at once to her aid. Another big tanker, the *Dextrous*, which had just completed a tow and might otherwise have steamed for the *Flying Enterprise*, went at once to take over the tow abandoned by the *Zwart Zee*, and with no other suitable tug immediately available Carlsen was faced with an indefinite period adrift.

Later that day, 30th December, Carlsen was told that the *Turmoil*, which was one of the biggest and fastest tugs afloat, would sail from Falmouth to assist him as soon as it had completed the tow of the Shell tanker. But it would be three or four days before it could reach him. He settled down as philosophically as he could to spending these days alone in his grotesquely tilted ship. The list had now sharpened to 60 degrees, sometimes rolling to 80, exposing the red paint of the keel. The men on board the *General Greeley* noted that the merchantman's rudder and starboard screw were now permanently visible, the rudder flapping freely from side to side. What must life be like for the man on board?

Carlsen was living in the radio cabin on the port or low side of the ship, to be near his long-range radio in case of emergency. Every two hours he climbed up to his own cabin on the high starboard side to operate a small voice radio which he had rigged there, to keep in touch with the *General Greeley* and its successor as escort, the *Golden Eagle*. His was a topsy-turvy world. He jammed a mattress in one corner of the radio cabin, wedged himself in, and slept there as best he could. As the ship rolled, the wall of the cabin levelled almost to the horizontal. He had no water, due to hydraulic failure, so he began a slow perilous crawl round the cabin-deck, collecting the water in the thermos flasks in each cabin. Slithering, scrambling, sliding, halling, he then made his way along the high starboard side of the ship to the store-room. All he could find when he got there was a huge cake, enough for the whole ship. It must have been one of the last things the cook made. It had a hole in the middle, which made it easy to carry, so he thrust an arm through it, carrying it on his wrist. He would need both hands for the scramble back to the cabin.

The heaving, slanting deck looked almost vertical. The rail on the far side, directly beneath him, was completely submerged now, the decks awash to the hatch coamings. If those hatches gave it would be the end.

He had no warmth or lighting in the radio cabin, apart from candles. More than anything he longed for a hot drink. He boiled water in a small can by the heat of a candle, and made tea. The fruit cake tasted good. For the next few days indeed, he had nothing but tea and cake. There was no news of the *Turmoil*. On his third morning alone he signalled Captain Donahue of the *Golden Eagle*. 'Good morning, and a Happy New Year to you.' It was 1st January, 1952.

Next day the *Golden Eagle* was replaced by the destroyer *John Weeks*. 'Wouldn't you be more comfortable if you crossed to the *Weeks*?' asked Captain Donahue before he left.

'Yah, that is correct.' Carlsen's Danish accent was strong. 'But I have valuable cargo on board. I can't leave it.'

On the following night, when Carlsen was in speech contact with the *Weeks*, he mentioned his personal needs for the first time. 'I wouldn't mind', he said, 'some hot coffee and meat sandwiches, and some magazines.' He only had one book in the cabin, entitled *The Seaman and the Law,* and he read and re-read it repeatedly.

Cautiously, because of the risk of collision, the destroyer closed in towards the wallowing *Flying Enterprise*, until the two ships were rising and falling on the same swell, not more than 40 yards apart. Balanced high on the hull, outside the starboard rail, stood Carlsen. Three times the American crew fired a line at him, and three times he failed to get it as the ship lurched. Eventually he went back to his radio. 'Let's wait till the weather abates,' he said. 'You fellows are taking a worse beating than I am.'

Meanwhile the *Turmoil* had completed its task and was steaming at full speed for the Atlantic, her heavy towing hawsers curled inboard. The gale was still blowing, hail was lashing the bridge, and Captain Dan Parker, the tug's master, unshaven and unchanged after seven days and nights on salvage work in the height of the storm, radioed that he did not expect to reach the scene before dark next day, 3rd January. Whether this would be in time to save the *Flying Enterprise* seemed doubtful. The weather in the Atlantic was better, but the barometer was falling.

Cable messages from all over the world were reaching Carlsen via the destroyer *Weeks*. Most of them urged him to leave. He had stayed on board his crippled ship until a salvage operation had been mounted by the owners. No one else could claim salvage rights now. It was time he thought of himself, or at least of his wife and family. One cable was from Hans Isbrandtsen, head of American Export Isbrandtsen Lines, the owners. 'A rescue ship is standing by,' it said. 'Put your own safety before that of the ship.' But the reply was terse. 'I am remaining until the vessel is towed into port, or sinks.'

During the morning the destroyer was able to pass food, cigarettes, coffee and magazines to Carlsen. The crew cheered as he collected them. He took them back to the radio cabin and had his first meal for a week. Never had sandwiches and coffee tasted so good.

The *Turmoil* was making 12 knots through strong winds and heavy seas. At dusk the tug's outline appeared on the horizon. But it was some hours after dark before it reached the *Flying Enterprise*. One look at the ship in his searchlights convinced Captain Parker that there was no time to be lost.

He must try to get her in tow that night. He established speech contact with Carlsen, and they agreed that as the freighter was down by the bows they would try to tow her stern first. It was decided that Parker should fire a messenger line aboard, which Carlsen would grab. Once Carlsen had secured the line the tug's winches would unroll the hawser. But Carlsen would have to work alone. It was too dangerous to attempt to put anyone else on board in the heavy seas.

Captain Parker brought the tug round to the stern of the freighter and fired the line. Carlsen, unable to support himself on the steeply sloping deck without hanging on with one hand, groped at the line with the other. He caught it and had almost secured it when it parted.

Buffeted in a 40-knot wind, drenched by every lurch and toss of his ship, Carlsen grabbed repeatedly at the messenger line. Four times his grab was successful, but each time, as he hauled in the rope, the movement of the two ships on the swell pulled the line suddenly taut and snapped it. When daylight came Parker signalled the *Weeks*, which closed in and spoke to Carlsen by loud hailer. 'Can you go up to the bows? It may be easier to secure the hawser there.'

Carlsen, already soaked and fatigued after his all-night efforts, set off on the 350-foot crawl and scramble along the starboard rail to the far end of his ship. All movement now was torture for him. The sloping deck had twisted his shoes into unrecognisable shape and the leather dug into his ankles, which were swollen and scarred under the strain. Even to stand immobile was painful. But at last he reached the bows, where Parker had already manoeuvred the *Turmoil*.

Four more efforts were made to secure a tow, all unsuccessful. Parker was now fighting against considerable sternway, so he decided to make another approach from aft. Back crawled Carlsen along the starboard rail. This time Parker tried a heavier, stronger line. Carlsen got it through the chocks and began hauling. Again the dancing movement of the ships tensed the line at a critical moment and snapped it. They tried a second time, and Carlsen had the hawser round a bollard and was within two feet of making it fast when the line snapped again.

Carlsen's muscles were numbed and feeble after 12 hours of continuous effort and he was in danger of being swept away. To conserve his strength he crawled back to the cabin and rested while the *Turmoil* rigged fresh gear. It was clear that for the moment he was all in. But Parker still did not consider attempting to put anyone else aboard. It was far too risky. Carlsen would regain his strength presently, and in any case the actual manual effort required to connect the towline was small.

Darkness had fallen before Parker was ready for a further attempt. The seas had moderated slightly, Carlsen was alerted, and this time Parker brought the stern of the tug right up under the stern of the freighter. As he was manoeuvring, the two ships were drawn together on the top of the swell, and for a brief moment they made the lightest of contacts. It was a moment, though, of unique opportunity.

Standing on the grating at the stern of the tug was the 27-year-old mate Kenneth Dancy. Almost directly above him he could see the stern of the freighter, tilted at a crazy angle. Suddenly a wave lifted the stern of the tug exactly level with the freighter. It was then that the vessels kissed. Entirely on impulse, Dancy caught the freighter's taffrail and swung himself aboard.

Carlsen stumbled across towards him. 'Welcome aboard the *Flying Enterprise*!'

'Shake hands!'

'I'm mighty pleased to see you!'

It was an emotional moment. But the seas had moderated only just long enough to give Dancy the chance to get aboard. Their combined efforts failed to secure the tow-line, and the gale soon made it impossible for them to stay on deck. For the rest of the night they sheltered in the radio

cabin. Carlsen cleared a space for Dancy and found him a
mattress. Soaked to the skin but wrapped in blankets, they
lay down to rest.

'Good-night Mr. Dancy.'

'Good-night Captain.'

All that night the ship creaked and groaned, while loose
gear clattered across the deck and the rudder grated to and
fro. Carlsen slept, but Dancy, nerve-racked by the incessant
noise and oppressed by claustrophobia, spent a restless night.

Next morning, Saturday 5th January, despite fog and
drizzle, they finally succeeded in making fast the hawser.
They shouted, cheered and waved—it was the grandest
moment of all. For Carlsen, all the risks and privations of the
past eight days seemed justified. For Dancy, who had re-
solved to stay with Carlsen and share his fate, the sacrifice
was suddenly worth while. Yet both men knew that the
actual tow would expose them to even greater dangers. Friction caused by the tugging might turn the freighter over.
One false move by Captain Parker would capsize them.
They were 350 miles from Falmouth, and they could not
hope to make more than three or four knots under tow. For
the next few days their lives would be a continual nightmare.

All the normal difficulties of towing in heavy seas would
be accentuated by the unstable nature of the tow. The
freighter would be a brute to handle. There was the ever-
present danger that the cable would 'snatch' and part under
the strain. Captain Parker hoped to prevent this by using a
long tow—nearly half a mile of cable. But worst of all was the
danger of chafing. In stormy seas and with a wallowing
weight on the end of the tow, hardly any gear would stand
up for long. If the hawser were severed, valuable time would
be lost in re-connecting. The freighter could not float for
ever. Yet with all these difficulties Parker and Carlsen were
hopeful, even confident. The main threat, as always at sea,
was the weather.

That night the wind dropped, the sea ran smoothly, and the tow went well. The *Flying Enterprise* was crabbing along at the end of her half-submerged tow-rope, sheering from quarter to quarter, progressing almost broadside on. 'I feel like a million dollars', signalled Carlsen, 'now she's in tow.' To lose his ship—that was the dread of the sea captain. But to have lived to see someone else bring it into port after he had abandoned it—that was a humiliation Carlsen could not have borne.

All day Sunday the tow went on. Parker hoped to reach Falmouth some time on Wednesday. But on Monday morning there were signs of a change in the weather. The wind stiffened and the seas were heavier. Even so, Parker kept the tow going steadily at $3\frac{1}{2}$ knots. By dawn on Tuesday, the fourth day of the tow, Falmouth was less than 100 miles away. The *Flying Enterprise,* her funnel and derricks almost parallel with the water, was riding well.

All day long, as the convoy steamed nearer and nearer to port, the excitement on land grew. Carlsen's parents were flown over from Copenhagen. The Danish naval attaché in London hurried down to Falmouth with a personal message from the King of Denmark. And Falmouth was *en fête*. Arcades of bunting festooned the streets, all vantage points overlooking the bay were claimed and the town was packed with cars. A civic reception was ready for Carlsen and Dancy.

Late that afternoon the convoy was less than 50 miles off the Lizard. So many aircraft were circling overhead that special flying control precautions had to be enforced to avert collision. A cluster of small ships steamed out to have a look at the freighter; everyone marvelled at the miracle that was keeping her afloat. Every time she dipped and rolled it seemed she must turn over. People on these little ships could see the water rushing up her decks, could stare into the open conning position on top of her bridge and peer straight down her funnel. All the time she was yawing from side to side, never pointing in the same direction for long. And there, high on a pile of sacks on the starboard side, sitting on the hull, were Carlsen and Dancy. It was an incredible sight, an epic which in a few hours would move to a triumphant climax in Falmouth harbour.

But the Atlantic had gathered itself for a final assault on the *Flying Enterprise*. The winds were building up again to gale force, the seas were angry and turgid, the tow-rope lashed at the water like some repressed reptile of the deep. Then the port lifeboat, skimming the water like a surfboard, was suddenly wrenched from its davits and hurled against the superstructure before being whirled away in the storm. Captain Parker, determined not to be cheated of his salvage at the last minute—he was on a 'no cure, no pay' contract—decided to heave to, easing the strain, riding out the storm. They were 27 miles south of the Scillies.

After four hours the sea began to moderate, and after six hours Parker began to take up the tow. He brought the drifting freighter slowly into wind and was under way again before midnight. Two hours later he signalled the Lizard. 'We are making $3\frac{1}{2}$ knots. Everything is going well.' It seemed that the sea had relented. But within a minute of this signal going out, the final disaster hit the *Flying Enterprise*.

Carlsen and Dancy were asleep in the radio cabin, and the *Turmoil* had to circle the freighter and sound its siren to wake them up. Carlsen climbed up to his radio. The message awaiting him was brief. 'The cable's gone.'

Carlsen's heart stopped, then thumped involuntarily. Although he did not admit it to himself he knew now that nothing short of a miracle could save his ship.

'We'll try again,' Parker was saying, 'and then again.' They must not give up hope. In the morning they would refix the tow. 'Get back to bed,' said Parker, 'there's nothing you can do till daylight.'

Carlsen slipped and skidded back to the radio cabin, fell back on his mattress, and forced himself back into a restless sleep. To exhaust himself with worry wouldn't help his ship. At dawn the two men crawled into the bows to survey the damage. The tow-line had chafed through near the chock. There was a quick-release shackle, but it had buckled under the strain. They would have to cut it free.

Using a hacksaw, they fought to sever the broken gear, struggling to keep their foothold on the slanting deck. Every pitch of the ship brought a wall of water crashing over them, every roll seemed bent on loosening their hold. Then an enormous wave broke over them. When it subsided, only one figure remained.

Carlsen had been knocked flat on his back and swept down the deck at avalanche speed. He found himself floundering in the sea far beyond the submerged port rail. Yet somehow he managed to swim back and rejoin Dancy in the bows.

It took them three hours to hack through the shackle. By the time the heavy gear slid across the deck and splashed into the sea, both men were exhausted. The seas were too rough for passing fresh gear. They crawled back to the cabin to dry out their clothes.

The *Flying Enterprise* was settling deeper. The sea was crashing into the radio cabin, forcing Carlsen and Dancy to move into the captain's cabin on the higher starboard side. There they propped themselves against a pile of displaced furniture, rigging an escape rope through the door to the starboard rail so they could climb the rope to safety if the ship capsized.

Next morning the winds were steady at gale force and there was no hope of getting a tow-line across. It was impossible for Carlsen and Dancy to get to either end of the ship. The *Turmoil* and the *Willard Keith,* an American destroyer which had relieved the *John Weeks,* continually urged the two men to leave before they were trapped. But Carlsen and Dancy, wrapped in blankets and with their clothes sodden, still hoped that the storm might abate. If it did, they could still be in Falmouth by nightfall. Surely the ship would float that long. But even Carlsen doubted it. He did not like the feel of her. Through the worn leather of his twisted shoes, through the soles of his blistered feet, he could feel his ship dying underneath him.

At two o'clock that afternoon he was in contact with the captain of the *Willard Keith*. 'Culdrose will send a helicopter to take you both off,' said Commander O'Brien, 'but they can only stay overhead for five minutes. You'll have to make a decision now. Will you leave?'

All other offers of this kind had been rejected by Carlsen. But now he hesitated. His ship was sinking. He had another man to think of. Yet an affirmative would be the final admission of defeat, to himself and to the world. He shrank from it. For some time he did not answer, and when he did his voice was unrecognisable.

'Yes.'

The helicopter took off from Culdrose.

Twenty minutes later Commander O'Brien was watching the helicopter on his radar screen, seven miles north of the *Flying Enterprise*. The pilot was feeling his way through buffeting winds and frustrating patches of low cloud. The pick-up was to be made on the starboard side, now virtually a flat surface.

Suddenly, under the pressure of air and water, the wheelhouse doors blew open. Carlsen called at once on his radio. 'It's no good, she won't last. We're coming out now.' They hauled themselves out of the cabin on the rope and scrambled down the side of the superstructure. There was no sign of the helicopter, but the pilot was calling the *Willard Keith*.

'I can't get through the cloud. I've reached my endurance limit. I shall have to go back.'

O'Brien called Parker on the *Turmoil*. 'The helicopter's turned back. We shall have to get those two off mighty quick.'

7a Hedley Cliff

7b The *Daisy*'s dinghy alongside the *Nella Dan*

7c Douglas Wardrop with his mother and sister after rescue

8a Captain Reeks   8b Mary Rogers

8c The *Stella*

The *Flying Enterprise* was going down. Her angle had slipped beyond 90 degrees and the sea was pouring into her funnel. Carlsen and Dancy were standing together in their lifejackets on the hull, waving to the *Turmoil*.

Carlsen pointed to the funnel, the starboard side of which was still clear of the water. 'Come on, Mr. Dancy. We'll walk off along the stack.'

'Right, Captain.'

Carlsen and his involuntary mate Dancy, who had never lapsed from the formal style of address, walked hand in hand along the horizontal funnel, swung their legs over the rim, and jumped. Even in the sea they still held hands. They had vowed to stick together. Ten minutes later they were both aboard the *Turmoil*.

The *Flying Enterprise* was in its death-throes. The masts were slapping the water, the deck cargo was floating away. She was going down stern first, it seemed, her bows lifted as if in a last dive. But then the stern came up again, lifting out of the ocean, dripping with water, before shuddering and sinking slowly back. The bows rose this time in morbid triumph, poised for the final plunge. But Kurt Carlsen did not see it. He did not see anything in those last few moments. Head bowed, eyes stinging, he turned away and was led silently below.

The subdued warmth of the welcome that Falmouth gave to Carlsen, Dancy and Parker next day compensated for the absence of gaiety. All but one of the freighter's complement had been rescued, yet the story seemed stark in its tragedy. For more than 300 miles the *Turmoil* had dragged the waterlogged freighter through storm and sea. It was an ironic, derisory twist that she should finally be lost when almost in sight of land.

For fourteen days the world had followed the tussle hour by hour. For fourteen days high affairs of state had been squeezed out of the news bulletins and pushed off the front pages, thrust from the public mind. During that time,

I

millions had shared in the hopes and doubts and fears of a hero, of two heroes, living with them through a microcosm of mans eternal struggle against his ancient friend and enemy the sea.

* * *

Kurt Carlsen is still sailing with American Export Isbrandtsen lines and is currently master of the S.S. *Exbrook*. Kenneth Dancy married a Dutch girl and after being master of a coastal tanker for a time he gave up the sea and took a shore job in Holland, where he now works for E.M.I. Captain Dan Parker had the misfortune in 1955 to fall off *Turmoil's* bridge on to the steel boat deck, and he died while being taken ashore in a launch.

'Had we been successful in bringing the *Flying Enterprise* safely to port,' writes Captain Harry Davis, former second officer of the *Turmoil* and now himself a tug master, 'I would have expected a bonus of about £30, but as the contract was on the basis of a Lloyd's Open Form (no cure, no pay), we could expect nothing. However, the Isbrandtsen line very generously awarded £2,500 to the *Turmoil*, stipulating that Captain Parker should get £750 and Kenneth Dancy £500, the balance to be shared amongst the crew according to rank. My share came to £66.'

I am indebted to Captain Davis for many other personal details, and especially for a correction to the story as it first appeared. All reports at the time stated that Kenneth Dancy's boarding of the freighter was a planned operation, but this was not so. 'The late Captain Parker never even considered putting a boarding party aboard the *Enterprise* by any means other than by boat, and he did not consider that risk necessary as very little manual effort would be required to make the towing connection. The method of securing the tow-line was to manoeuvre the tug close to the listing side of the stern of the *Enterprise*, and pass the bight of a $2\frac{1}{2}$ inch (circ.) rope through the mooring lead and round the mooring bollard. All further heaving would be done by the tug's capstan. It was while doing this that the *Turmoil* and *Enterprise* drew together on top of the swell and actually touched very lightly. Ken Dancy happened to be standing on the grating at the stern of the tug, and as the ships touched he caught the rails on the stern of the *Enterprise* and swung himself aboard, but it was certainly not planned to board in that manner.'

It was quite by chance that Kenneth Dancy was aboard the *Turmoil* at all. The regular chief officer had had to attend a court of enquiry into an earlier disaster and Dancy was engaged to replace him. He had had no previous experience of salvage work.

8

Island Nightmare

The man at the oars of the tiny plywood dinghy was facing a problem. He had rowed across the 800-yard Passe Percée separating Jethou, smallest and loveliest of the Channel Islands, from the island of Herm, off Guernsey; but approaching the steep, rocky coast of Herm he was finding the current strong—too strong, it seemed, for him to reach the landing steps less than 50 yards away. 'Pull hard on your left oar,' said his companion, facing him in the stern less than three feet away. 'We're being swept south.'

Looking back over his right shoulder the rower saw that they were quite a way down from the steps. He started to pull harder and to increase his rate, but he seemed to be making little impression. Close into the shore the current was racing. He decided to pull out into slacker water, then make up to a point above the steps and let the tide carry them in. If that didn't work they would have to give up and go back to Jethou.

He began to manoeuvre the dinghy out of the current. 'I'm getting wet back here,' said his companion. He was a big man, and his weight in the stern was giving only inches of freeboard, so that every wave slopped over his seat. 'I'll give you a hand on the oars.' And he began to lean forward. At the first movement he made the little pram dinghy, only six feet long, rocked perilously, then capsized. Both men were tipped straight out into the water.

'I hope to God you can swim.'

The man who had been at the oars was a retired group captain named Hedley Cliff, aged 48, whose life had familiarised him with the sea. Working for the most of his R.A.F. service alongside the Navy, he had led many anti-shipping

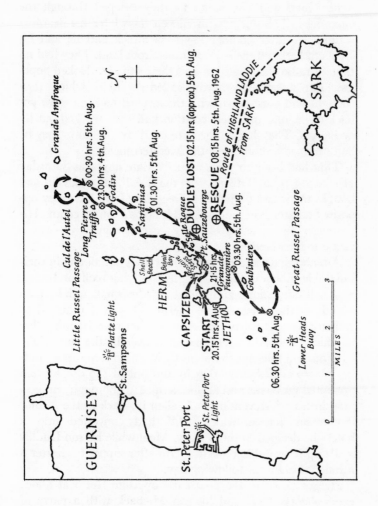

strikes, including the main Beaufort torpedo attack on the *Scharnhorst* and *Gneisenau* as they escaped through the Channel in February 1942. Eleven days later his Beaufort caught fire after another low-level attack and he and his crew crashed into the sea 200 miles from land. They had no time to radio their position and their situation looked hopeless. But a homing pigeon called 'Winkie' which they thought had gone down with the aircraft had somehow got back to its loft, and their position had been worked out by deduction. They had all been rescued. In the same year he had survived a ditching in the Mediterranean.

That had been 20 years ago: the date now was Saturday 4th August 1962. Retiring from the R.A.F. in 1958, Cliff had bought the island of Jethou, three miles from Guernsey opposite St. Peter Port, and opened it up as a tourist centre. His passenger this evening—Dudley Attenborough, 52—was a visitor to the island.

Attenborough and his father had been out all day in their inflatable rubber outboard dinghy, studying rock formations and collecting flora and fauna on the small uninhabited islands to the north-east of Herm. They had returned to Jethou about six-thirty that evening after an exhausting day in which they had been somewhat shaken by the force of the currents and tide-rips to the north. With no recognised landing places available, getting in and out of the dinghy had presented problems and at one point Attenborough senior, a man in his mid-seventies, had fallen in. Back at the Manor House on Jethou—which Cliff had converted into a hotel—he decided to retire early. Meanwhile his son Dudley made up his mind to cross to Herm after supper to charter a fishing vessel for the following day.

He got down to the boathouse opposite Herm at about eight o'clock. Cliff and his son Michael, with a party of Michael's friends, were already there, cleaning up the licensed café near the boathouse after the day's influx of visitors, then relaxing and having a drink. Cliff and his son helped Attenborough launch the rubber dinghy, but the motor refused to start. Attenborough was obviously distressed. 'If you must go,' said Cliff, 'I'll row you across.'

It was a fine summer evening, about half-tide up, with a steady breeze blowing from the north-west. The waters around the islands are notorious for their tide rips, but Cliff was used to them and had rowed across to Herm before. He judged that the tidal current from the Jethou landing stage would be flowing towards Herm, taking them comfortably across the Passe Percée. Once they reached the slack water on the far side of the channel they would be able to make up to the Rosaire steps.

'We'll be back in about two hours,' Cliff told his son. 'Tell your mother where I am. And leave the light on in the pub to guide us.' Attenborough seated himself in the stern, and at about 8.30 they set off across the Passe Percée. Michael Cliff watched them go.

After the shock of the immersion both men recovered quickly. 'Yes, I'm O.K.,' said Attenborough. He knew boats and was a good swimmer. 'Help me turn the dinghy upside down, then,' said Cliff. The sinking, waterlogged dinghy would be useless to them as a support, but if they could turn it upside down quickly and trap some air underneath, it would make a stable platform for them to hang on to.

'That's better,' said Cliff, as the dinghy turned bottom uppermost. 'Now grab the oars.' He thought they might come in handy. 'We'll try to float down to the Percée rock. Let's hope somebody saw us.' In fact, Michael Cliff had gone back to the bar in the café. No one had seen them capsize.

'Ought we to swim for it?'

'No. If we couldn't get a hold ashore we'd have had it. And if anyone's looking for us it's best to stay with the boat.'

It was getting dark now, and Attenborough had a torch which he flashed at the landing stage on Jethou and up towards the landing steps on Herm. But the light was not seen.

So began a nightmare voyage around the rocks and islets of the Channel Islands, a voyage in which the little up-turned boat would be totally at the mercy of tide, current, wind and whirlpool.

The speed of the current was astonishing. They could see that they were being swept past the Perceé rock and down towards the Point-de-Sauzebourg on the south-east corner of Herm. 'Our best bet', said Cliff, 'is to let the tide take us round the point. Then we can swim ashore on the south coast of Herm.' Attenborough agreed.

Clinging precariously to the upturned dinghy as it swirled and pirouetted in the tide-race, both men realised that they were liable to be thrown off at any moment. Somehow they had to steady the dinghy and improve their hold. The bottom of the dinghy was smooth plywood, but a thin batten an inch deep down the 'keel' gave them a minimum grip with their fingers. Streaming their legs out astern, they crooked the paddle poles under their armpits and crossed the blades on the upturned bow, pressing them down for balance and support. This left them free to kick their legs to maintain a limited control.

Cliff's watch was still working and he noted that they rounded the Point-de-Sauzebourg at 9.15. Soon they saw the granite mass of Selle Roque looming out of the dusk straight ahead. They were close in to Herm and would pass between the island and the rock. There was no chance of getting ashore here, but while they stayed so close to Herm an opportunity would come.

It was Attenborough who took over now, pointing out their likely direction of drift, identifying rock formations by name, judging their prospects. He knew these waters well.

'What do you think we should do?'

'Hang on for a bit,' said Attenborough. 'It's far too rough here, and too steep as well. We'd never be able to climb out.'

'Where do you think we'll end up?'

'The tide will take us along past Belvoir Bay. It should be easy to swim ashore there.'

They had passed inside Selle Roque, but the next two rocks went by on their left; they were being swept north-east, through the overfalls and outcrops of rock to the south-east of Herm. If this went on they would miss Belvoir Bay. Their efforts to steer the boat against the tide race were not very successful. Then their direction veered and they were swept north again along the Bay.

There was a light on in the beach café, and they measured the distance to it, evaluating the swim. The tide had taken them too far out.

At eleven o'clock they were a mile off Shell Beach, to the north of Belvoir Bay, still hanging on hopefully, looking for a chance to get ashore. But the currents and overfalls were still too powerful. Even the boat itself seemed in constant danger now as they swirled and raced straight for huge lumps of granite that it seemed they must smash into. The thin plywood dinghy would never withstand such a collision.

Looming out of the darkness they saw the islets of Sardinias and Godin straight ahead. If they could have controlled their direction they might have got ashore on Godin, with its sandy beach, but instead they found themselves heading for more rocks. Yet like flotsam in a swollen river they repeatedly swerved past obstacles and continued on their course.

On they went, past the rocky islets of Traiffe and then Longue Pierre, its tall granite stack standing out against the sky. Over to port Cliff could see a lighthouse flashing, and he recognised it as Platte Fougère, off St. Sampson's, the commercial port on Guernsey. That meant they were now north of Herm. Then as they careered still further north the lights of the coast road running south to St. Peter Port came into view one by one, and finally St. Peter Port itself, with its beacon and the climbing neon lights of the town. They were a good five miles away.

'We're heading for Grand Amfroque,' said Attenborough,

'or Cul l'Autel. To think I only left there about eleven hours ago.' These were the northernmost rocks of the group, the furthest point reached by Attenborough and his father earlier in the day. Beyond them lay the open sea.

'We'll be carried right out into the Channel,' said Cliff.

'Yes—but the tide should turn soon after midnight. If we're not taken too far that should carry us back.'

Cliff had been conscious of a distant roaring sound in his ears for some minutes. Now it was getting closer. 'What the hell's that?'

'That's the surf breaking on Autel rock. God help us if we get caught there. The current rips through there like a river in spate.'

Looking northwards Cliff saw a grey-white shape looming up out of the darkness 400 yards ahead, more eerie even than the sound of the roaring. It was Autel rock. Layer upon layer of birdlime was making it shine a luminous white in the starlight. 'I doubt if we'll be able to get on it, said Attenborough. 'It's too slippery. And if we miss it we'll soon be out in mid-Channel.' The nearest land to the north-east was the Cherbourg peninsula, 30 miles away.

The roaring and sucking of the surf got louder and more sibilant, the sea became rougher, and they seemed to be bearing straight down on the rock. Then the dinghy steadied slightly and they found they were drifting slowly past, leaving the rock on their starboard side.

As the current took them round to the north-east of Autel their view of Guernsey was interrupted and they could no longer orientate themselves by the lights. For a time they lost their bearings and were uncertain of their direction of drift. Then, half an hour after midnight, the lights of Guernsey appeared again, this time to the left of Autel. The tide had turned and they were moving back south.

'This is fine,' said Attenborough. 'We might have better luck this way. We might hit Godin. If not we should finish up somewhere in Belvoir Bay.' They were much more cheerful now, yet Cliff noticed that Attenborough sounded breathless.

'Are you all right?'

'Tired.'

Cliff helped him forward along the dinghy. 'Try to get nearer the middle.' They had been immersed for over four hours, and in these fast-moving currents the water was always cold. The hull of the dinghy was three-parts under water all the time, and only about a foot of the narrow bow end showed clear.

They soon realised they were going to miss Godin. They were farther out from the rocks than they had been on the way up, though they were still heading south-west for Herm. Ahead of them were some outlying lumps of granite which would be impossible to cling to, and here the sea roughened and the overfalls multiplied, breaking at times over their heads. From time to time they swallowed water as they were caught unawares. 'I'm getting very tired,' said Attenborough. The long day he had had amongst the islands was beginning to tell on him. 'I'm slipping.'

In the cross-currents and eddies near the rocks the dinghy swirled violently and Attenborough was jerked off. Cliff just managed to grab a handful of his guernsey pullover as he went, hold on, and somehow drag him back. 'Get astride the hull,' Cliff told him. 'Straddle it.' And he helped Attenborough to a more secure position. Then he swam round to the bow himself, and hung on there. Cliff had retained his oar, but Attenborough had lost his.

The lights of Guernsey were hidden again now behind Herm, but they illuminated the island's skyline. The dinghy was still much farther out than on the way up and Cliff could see that they would be carried beyond Belvoir Bay. He could see the lighthouse flashing now on Sark, four of five miles to port. Then their course changed again and they began to head in towards Selle Roque. The change was too late to wash them on to Herm, but if they held this new direction they would finish up back on Jethou.

Nearing Selle Roque the whirlpool of cross-currents twisted and twirled the dinghy so viciously that it seemed certain they would crash into the rock. Cliff saw Attenborough slither off the boat into the water. He thrust his oar towards him and Attenborough grabbed at it, but as he did so the dinghy spun savagely in yet another whirlpool. When it steadied Cliff looked around for Attenborough, but he was gone. With only one man now clinging to it, the upturned dinghy swept on into the night.

When Cliff next looked at his watch the time was 3.30 and the first hint of dawn was in the sky. The tide had taken him south of Herm and he was passing Jethou, too far out to swim ashore. Somebody might see him, though—surely the alarm would have been raised by now.

Michael Cliff and his friends had left the café soon after eleven o'clock. The wind had stiffened and the water separating the island from Herm was rough and corrugated. It looked as though his father had decided to spend the night on Herm. Back at the house, Margaret Cliff was not greatly concerned at her husband's non-appearance; she had come to the same conclusion. There was no telephone link between Jethou and Herm, otherwise she would have put a call through. She waited up until two o'clock just in case, then went to bed.

The dinghy was still being swept southwards, past Jethou and Fauconnière and on past the Goubinière rock in the Great Russel. Cliff thought he could have swum to Goubinière, he was so close to it, but it rose sheer from the sea and he could see no handholds.

The morning star was shining with unusual brilliance, and

he remembered the last time he had seen it, sitting in a rubber dinghy in the North Sea. Dawn was giving all the promise of a beautiful August day.

The sun was up now and he could see the harbour wall of St. Peter Port three miles or more to the north-west. He was being carried down towards the cluster of low-lying rocks at the southern extremity of the group. He thought he would be able to get on to one of these. They were overlooked by the watch-tower on the main jetty, and with luck someone might see him through the glasses. Then he realised he was being carried past them, leaving them well to starboard.

He must be heading straight for the Lower Heads Buoy, the buoy at the entrance to the Little Russel which all shipping to and from Jersey and the south must pass. The mail steamer from England would be in St. Peter Port soon, and during the morning it would leave for Jersey. If he could get on to that buoy it would pass right by him. There was the Sark ferry, too—that usually sailed via the Lower Heads Buoy. He could just see the buoy now, perhaps half a mile away, and presently he heard the mournful clanging of its bell. He couldn't see the mail steamer, but it might well have arrived already and be unloading inside the harbour.

He had forgotten that it was Sunday morning. There were no mail steamers on a Sunday, nor was there a Sark ferry.

The morning breeze was chill and he found that by submerging completely every few minutes he could keep much warmer. He took up his original position astern, kicking out his legs to improve his circulation. He seemed to be completely numb from the waist down.

He could still see the buoy, but it didn't seem to be getting any closer. It was still too far to swim. Then he noticed that the rocks to starboard were receding. The time was seven o'clock and the tide had turned again.

He was out in the Great Russel now, half-way between Guernsey and Sark. The tide was taking him north-east again, but much farther out from the islands this time. There was no hope of being carried ashore from here. By the time he drifted back on the next tide—if he could last that long—he would be nearer Sark.

He had never seen the islands look so lovely. The sky was almost cloudless, the air was crystal clear, and the sea was calm now, and bluer than he'd ever known. The trees on the long slope of Herm stood out in sharp relief, and the patches of cultivation looked incredibly green. Even the granite rocks looked peaceful now, their tide-rips distant and unseen.

His mind was only a little numb, and he could appreciate the beauty of the scene. He felt no fear. He had been born with a caul—something that his mother had always had implicit faith in—and he remembered her confidence now. He had made up his mind that the next tide would carry him down to Sark. He would hold on till then. He still had complete confidence in rescue.

He had let go of his oar, but he couldn't remember when. He just hadn't noticed it. It didn't strike him that some time in the next hour or so he was likely to loosen his grip on the dinghy in much the same way.

Drifting down the middle of the Great Russel on a Sunday morning after twelve hours in the water, his chances now were practically nil. Even the fishing boats wouldn't be out on a Sunday. The only vessel to pass through the Great Russel that morning had been a yacht that had been anchored the night before in Belvoir Bay; but he hadn't seen it. One of the crew had noticed a floating oar but had thought nothing of it.

The trouble was that the alarm had still not been given. When Michael Cliff got down to the boathouse that morning he saw that the tide was out, leaving the landing stage on Jethou high and dry. This was quite sufficient explanation for the continued absence of his father.

Yet some at least of the physical factors necessary to make rescue feasible were present. Visibility was good, and the sun was glinting on the varnished under-surface of the dinghy as it drifted northwards. If anyone came within a mile or so of it they would probably see it. Whether they would investigate was another matter.

Alf Taylor, a Guernsey fisherman who operated small boats to and from Sark in the summer, hadn't had a charter on a Sunday that year. But he had one this morning. A Sark family named Elliott wanted to get over to Guernsey in time to catch the midday plane for London, and as they had one or two calls to make first in Guernsey they wanted to start early. Taylor, in his open passenger launch *Highland Laddie*, had left St. Peter Port at 6.30, just about the time when Cliff was within sight of the Lower Heads Buoy. But Taylor had used the Bar Passage south of Jethou. He had been some way north of the drifting dinghy, too far to see it with the naked eye.

Taylor was due to pick up the Elliotts on Sark at 7.30 and he got there on time. The Elliotts were on the quay to meet him. If he got away at once, and if he chose the same route back, he might just possibly pass close enough to the drifting dinghy to see it.

Taylor saw no reason, on such a perfect morning, to take anything but the shortest route. His passengers, too, were anxious to get to Guernsey as soon as possible. The *Highland Laddie* left Sark at 7.35 by the northern route and headed across the Great Russel for Jethou.

Born in Alderney, Alf Taylor was a big, good-humoured man who knew the islands and every boat that sailed around them intimately. And even more important, he had good eyesight and an enquiring mind. When, half-way across the Great Russel, he saw something glinting in the sun about a mile to the north, he was curious.

The speck on the water looked like a lobster marker. As a fisherman he was always on the look-out for flotsam of that kind. 'Do you mind if we take a look at that?' he asked his passengers.

'What is it?'

'I don't know. Looks like a lobster bobber.'

'How long will it take?'

'About twenty minutes.'

The Elliotts hesitated. They were reluctant, but as they were well on time perhaps a short delay wouldn't matter. Eventually they agreed.

At a distance of 400 yards Taylor and the Elliotts realised that the object they were approaching was an upturned dinghy. It must have broken loose from its moorings. Taylor decided to keep going now and pick it up if he could. It must belong to someone. He was closing in on it when the Elliotts, standing up in the bows, shouted back to Taylor, 'There's a man clinging to it!'

Cliff had not seen the boat. It was only twenty yards away when he heard someone shouting 'Hang on! Hang on!' Then he looked up and saw it. His confidence in rescue had been miraculously justified.

As they pulled him out he told them that one man was missing, and he gave them the approximate location—near Selle Roque. Then he passed out. Taylor's estimate—and he was an ex-Naval man who had spent the war at sea—was that he might have lasted another twenty minutes.

Leaving the dinghy behind, Taylor sent a message on his ship-to-shore radio, and the lifeboat and an ambulance ship were sent out within minutes. They searched an extensive area off Jethou and Herm in vain. A fortnight later Attenborough's body was washed up near Selle Roque, very near the spot where he had disappeared.

The dinghy found its way back to Jethou three weeks later, stranding itself less than 50 yards from the point where Cliff and Attenborough had started out.

* * *

I had already written about two of the highlights in Hedley Cliff's life—the pigeon rescue in *Down in the Drink* and the main Beaufort attack on the *Scharnhorst* and *Gneisenau* as they passed through the Channel in 1942 in *The Ship-Busters*, so this was the third time I had written about him. As always he helped me most generously. He was one of those indestructible characters who always seem to come through, and it was a shock to hear of his death in Guernsey in 1969 at the age of 55.

9

Howard Blackburn and his Dory Mate

It was in the second half of January 1883 in a typically bleak winter that the schooner *Grace L. Fears* of Gloucester, Massachusetts called at the quiet port of Liverpool, Nova Scotia, to put a sick man ashore. Her skipper, Captain Alec Griffen, looked around for a replacement. As part of his equipment he carried six 17-foot dories, and one of his fishermen, a youngster without much experience named Tom Welch, was left without a dory mate.

It happened that a blue-eyed Gloucester fisherman of heavyweight build, more than six feet tall, was visiting his family in the adjacent village of Port Medway, where 25 years earlier he had been born. Howard Blackburn, a robust fellow with the gentle toughness that sometimes goes with powerful physique, had left home in his teens and gone to Gloucester, where for the past ten years he had made his living as a dory mate.

The elegant lines and square-rigged sail of the schooner attracted the interest of Blackburn and when he heard that she came from his adopted home-town he strode with firm but unhurried gait into Liverpool and made his way to the docks.

The only man he knew on board was the skipper, Captain Griffen. Griffen was delighted to see him. Blackburn was known as a man who literally pulled his weight, besides being considerate and unselfish—essential qualities for a dory mate. Men thrown together in a tiny boat in the capricious Atlantic needed to think instinctively not of themselves but of each other. Blackburn was a man who had these instincts.

'I've had to disembark a sick man,' said Captain Griffen, 'and I'm on my way to the Grand Banks. How about taking his place?'

The arrival of the schooner, and the unexpected vacancy in her crew, suited Blackburn well. He had been on the point of returning to Gloucester, and this would kill two birds with one stone. He signed on at once and sailed the same day.

Three days later the *Grace L. Fears* reached the Burgeo Bank, off southern Newfoundland, and next morning the six dories were lowered into the water and the dory-men rowed out across the bank to set their trawls. It was a hard pull, against the wind, but in the intense cold they were glad of it. When they stopped to lay their trawls, all that saved their hands from quick and certain frostbite was the pair of thick woollen mittens worn by each man.

Blackburn and his mate, Tom Welch, found an anchorage to hold the trawl to the sea-bed, laid the trawl, and set a surface buoy to mark it. Then they rowed back to the schooner. They were greeted by a worried-looking Captain Griffen. 'There's a blizzard coming up,' called Griffen. 'That's what it looks like to me. You'd better go right back and haul in the trawls.'

Blackburn and Welch, and the other ten dory-men, turned about and rowed out to sea again. Eventually they reached the outermost buoy, which they knew was their own. They began to haul in the trawl. As they did so, the wind fell away to a flat calm.

'I don't like it,' Blackburn told Welch, 'the wind'll probably turn against us now.' He was not surprised when, a few minutes later, just as they hauled in the last of the trawl, the wind breezed up from the north-west, immediately behind the schooner. They would have to row back into the teeth of the blizzard.

They could see the other five dories, already well on their way back to the schooner. The other dory-men had found closer anchorages and had not had so far to pull to regain their trawls. Soon they lost sight of them, and eventually even the twin masts of the schooner disappeared into the vaporous snow.

'Never mind,' said Blackburn, 'we've got her position. We'll keep rowing until we get to wind'ard of her. We shall hear her fog-horn by then.'

Five of the dories had reached the schooner before the worst of the blizzard, and the crew were peering helplessly for the sixth. Captain Griffen was sounding his fog-horn continually, but for Blackburn and Welch the sibilant clamour of the gale and the seas drowned all other sound. The snow had dropped an opaque curtain around them and they were deafened by the elements. In a few hours another curtain would fall on them—the curtain of night.

Blackburn and Welch pulled steadily, confident of their strength and sense of direction. Surely they must be abreast of the schooner by now. But they couldn't hear her fog-horn. That might mean that they had gone past her.

'We'll have to anchor, Tom,' said Blackburn.

'You're right.'

Night was falling with incredible swiftness and the only thing to do was to stay where they were and wait for daylight, hoping that by then the weather would clear. During the night it stopped snowing, and suddenly they saw the schooner.

'Look Tom! The light! There she is!'

Welcome as the discovery was it chilled them to find that they were still several miles downwind of the schooner. It seemed that in half a day's rowing they had made no progress at all. 'Come on,' said Blackburn, 'we've got to row for her. Another blizzard and we'll never find her.'

They were rowing for their lives now, and they knew it. But the riding light of the *Grace L. Fears* still receded. 'We shall have to drop anchor again,' said Blackburn. 'We're losing ground. We'll have to wait until this gale blows itself out.' When morning came there was no sign of the *Grace L. Fears*.

They were stranded in the Atlantic, 60 or 70 miles from the nearest land, in a tiny rowing-boat that was shipping water all the time. The cold was intensifying and it was still blowing hard. The dory wouldn't last much longer at anchor. They would have to ease the strain by putting it to a drag. That meant they would drift still further from land.

First they had to improvise a drag-anchor. They smashed in the head of one of the trawl-buoys, then tied the painter inside it. To secure the knot, Blackburn had to take off his mittens. He tucked them carefully under the thwart and set about tying the knots. As he did so, a heavy sea broke over the dory and swamped it.

Welch worked hard with the shovel-like scoop provided as a bale but he could make little impression on the quantity of sea that slopped about in the waterlogged dory. Blackburn grabbed a keg that they had intended to use as a buoy and knocked off the head, passing it to Welch to bale with while he launched the drag. They drifted more than they had at anchor, but it was not so hard on the frail dory.

Blackburn looked down at his hands. The mittens. He had forgotten about his mittens. He reached down under the thwart, feeling for them, but they were gone. 'Stop baling, Tom. My mittens. I took them off to tie the painter. They're somewhere in the boat.'

The water slapped and clucked against the inside of the dory. There was no sign of the mittens. They had been baled out or washed overboard. Welch sat for a moment as still as a statue, aware of what he had done. 'Your hands, Howard, your hands,' he kept saying. 'Look at your hands.'

'It wasn't your fault, Tom,' said Blackburn. 'How were you to know?'

Welsh was still staring at Blackburn's hands. The implications of their pale bloodlessness were just as serious for him.

Blackburn's mind worked quickly. In a few minutes his

hands would be frozen stiff, so stiff that he would no longer be able to row. They must be nearly a hundred miles from land. What use would he be to his dory mate if he couldn't row?

He had a vision of Tom Welch rowing for the shore with no hope of getting there, while he sat helplessly on the thwart, staring at his useless hands. Was there anything he could do about it? He thought there might be. If his hands were going to freeze solid—as they certainly were—why not grab the oars now and let the knuckles freeze round them, like a clench? Then all he would have to do would be to fit the oars into the frozen sockets when he wanted to row.

He took the blades and curled his fingers round them tightly. Already they were stiffening, and he had to shape each hand with the help of the other, pressing them hard round the oar-handle. He sat there with a strange detachment, watching his fingers lock into position, one from which he knew they would never move again.

He squeezed his fingers round the handles and held them there until he could no longer move them at all. He knew then that they were frozen stiff. It was safe now to slip them off the oar-handles and carry on as best he could with the immediate tasks of baling, and of breaking off the ice which was rapidly forming inside the dory. He did not think or worry any more about his hands. All that concerned him was that he would be able to do his bit as a dory mate.

He grabbed the gobstick—the stick they hit the big halibut with to kill them—wedged it in his clenched right hand, and started pounding away at the ice which lined the dory. Already it was making the boat heavy. They had to do something to lighten it quickly, and they dropped the trawls overboard together with all the fish they had caught except a 20lb chicken halibut, which they thought they might eat in emergency.

All that day Blackburn took his turn with Welch at breaking off the ice and baling out the dory. It was no good attempting to row until the sea was calmer. Towards night-fall, after a long spell of baling, Blackburn settled down in the bow beside Welch to rest. Almost at once a big sea broke over them, flooding the dory. Blackburn sat up, expecting Welch to do the same, but he did not move.

'Come on, Tom,' he called, 'quick, jump to it, man, or she'll sink.'

Blackburn seized the keg baler and began baling en-ergetically. Another sea like that would finish them. There was more than enough work for two men, but still Welch did not move.

'Come along, Tom,' urged Blackburn, 'don't give in, you must do your part.' He held up his misshapen hands, from which the skin was already peeling, the little finger of the right hand almost severed. 'Look at my hands, Tom. You can't be as bad as I am. Come on.'

But Welch did not move. 'What's the use, Howard? We can't last till morning. We might as well go first as last.' He lay listlessly in the bow of the dory, a beaten man.

The stark truth of what Welch said roused something in Blackburn—some deep-seated obstinacy that determined him to survive. Hour after hour he kept baling and pounding the ice, and when at last he realised he was about to collapse from exhaustion he went aft and sat in the bottom of the dory with his back to the wind, moving the thwart back and forth to keep himself awake. To sleep, he knew, was certain death.

Repeatedly through the night he tried to rouse Welch. 'Tom,' he shouted, 'Tom, you've got to keep going. You've got to keep awake.' But Blackburn could get no response from him other than an occasional subdued muttering which sounded like a prayer. Towards morning he called him and not no reply. He went forward, grasped him by the shoulders and shook him. He was dead.

For a moment he could not believe it. Only a few hours earlier Welch had seemed so strong, yet all the time he must have been the weaker of the two. He bitterly regretted now his words of reproach to his dory mate.

Blackburn lifted the body, waited for a moment of calm, and carried it aft, laying it down in the stern. He took off the dead man's mittens, but his own hands were so bruised and swollen that he could not get them on. Soon, as the freezing spray covered Welch's body, it became completely encased in ice.

Blackburn crouched now in the bow, waiting for daylight and a sight, as he hoped, of the schooner. But when daylight eventually came the horizon was empty. He knew they must have drifted many miles in the night. Captain Griffen and the *Grace L. Fears* could not stay at anchor for ever, and already he and Welch had probably been given up. He might have more than a hundred miles to row to reach land.

Soon after daybreak the seas moderated and the wind dropped. Blackburn hauled in the drag-anchor, slipped his bloated hands over the oar-handles, and started to row for the shore. He would have to keep alive through at least two more freezing days and nights to have any hope of getting there.

The friction of the oar-handles began to wear away the flesh on his frostbitten hands, but he had firmed his knuckles so tightly that the loss of flesh did not seriously relax his grasp. He could feel nothing, but throughout the daylight hours he watched his hands slowly deteriorating. There was no one now to bale the dory, but the sea remained calm and he shipped little water. Apart from one or two short spells with the keg baler he rowed all day. Fortunately he did not have to worry about niceties of direction. The coast of southern Newfoundland ran in a straight line at right angles to his course. All he had to do was steer as near as he could due north.

When night came he put out the drag again and lay to until morning, resting his body and limbs but setting his mind firmly against sleep. At daybreak he hauled in the drag and began to row again for the shore.

This was his third day at sea in the dory, and his second day of rowing alone. By dropping Welch's body overboard he could have lightened his task, but such a thought did not occur to him. Dead or alive, Tom Welch was his dory mate and he would get him back to the shore.

The end of the third day came and still there was no sign of land. But next morning he sighted a tiny white speck on the horizon. It was a small island, covered with snow. But there was no harbour, and not a single building of any kind. Even in summer it must be uninhabited. That meant almost certainly that there was no fresh water, so it was no good stopping there.

It was about noon when he made his landfall. The cliffs were so white and high that he was surprised he hadn't seen them before. He noticed a narrow fissure in the cliffs, then recognised the opening as the mouth of a small river and pulled towards it. He knew it must be a river because he could see the fresh water lying black and motionless on the surface of the sea.

On the far bank of the river, facing the sea, he could make out a wharf and a fisherman's hut. Everything was half-buried in a blanket of snow and the wharf and hut looked abandoned and derelict. But the current was strong, and soon he had to abandon his efforts to row up-river. He aimed for the wharf.

He imagined he could see people now, and when he examined their faces he found that he knew them. They were old friends, familiar faces, and they were laughing at him. They were laughing at his efforts to row up-river. Puzzled, he focused once more on the wharf. It was utterly deserted again, void and still.

He could hear voices now, calling to him, sometimes encouraging him, sometimes jeering at his efforts to pull across to the wharf. He tried to close his mind to them, but his eardrums filled with sound. At last he reached a flat rock at the outer end of the wharf. He stepped on to the rock and somehow dragged the stern of the dory after him until it lay almost clear of the water on the rock. Then he secured the painter and clambered up on to the wharf.

Night was upon him and he decided to take what shelter he could in the hut. It was little enough. There were holes in the roof, the doors had rotted away, and the snow had drifted in and covered the floor to a depth of eighteen inches. In one corner of the hut was a bed, just a board supported by blocks, also covered in snow. He turned the board over, found an old fish net for a pillow, and lay down, intending to rest but not to sleep. Almost at once he found himself losing consciousness.

He knew that he still mustn't sleep. He got up and dragged himself round the hut all night, trampling down the snow. In the morning he went back to the dory, but when he reached it he found that the sea had pounded it all night on the rock, knocking out the bottom plug and stoving a hole in one of the planks. The only thing still left inside was the body of Tom Welch. The oars and thwarts had been thrown out. At first he thought they had been carried away, then he saw them floating around in the water under the wharf.

He reached for the gaff and dug it through the instep of Welch's rubber boot, intending to lift him out. He had almost dragged him on to the wharf when the gaff slipped through his hands and the body slithered off the bank and sank in about twelve feet of water.

He would have to pull the dory further up the rock if he was going to make it seaworthy. But he could not pull it with his hands. He gripped the painter with his teeth, and each time a wave lifted the dory a few inches up the rock he took up the slack with his teeth. In this way he managed at last to get the dory clear of the water. Then he did what he could to repair it.

He climbed back into the dory, shoved it off the rock with

his elbows, fished out the oars, slid them through his knuckles, and once again began to row. Instinctively he rowed east, some recess of memory telling him that he was more likely to find a village in that direction. Soon he saw a cluster of huts nestling together in a tiny cove. He pulled right into the cove. But there was no sign of life. He had made a mistake in leaving the river. In a few hours the tide and currents might be less powerful and he might be able to row up-river. There lay the best chance of finding food, fresh water, and habitation.

Slivers of his fingers and hands were being ground off all the time by the oar-handles. At first it seemed that the handles were contracting, but this could not be so. They were slipping about under his knuckles because he was gripping them now with bone and muscle alone. But he did not give up. He pulled steadily westwards along the coast until he regained the river.

He remembered now what he had to do. To and fro across the river, like a ship tacking, taking advantage of the eddies, avoiding the worst of the current. Each time he reached an eddy he stopped long enough to bale out the dory, then slid his hands over the oars again and began to row. After about two hours of this he found he was trying to row through solid ice.

He tied the dory to the bank and set off inland along the ice. How many paces he had gone he did not know, but suddenly he seemed to be surrounded by people—people and dogs. The faces of the people were unfamiliar this time. Were they any more real than the faces he had seen on the wharf?

Questions were being fired at him from all sides. 'Where have you come from? What do you want? Look at your hands! Oh, your poor hands! Come into the house and we'll bandage them.'

He had stumbled on a settlement, and every man, woman and dog had come out on to the ice to meet him. But all he could think of was Tom Welch, his dory mate, lying in twelve feet of water at the bottom of the wharf.

'I can't come with you now. I've got to go back for my dory mate.'

'Where is he?'

'He's lying in twelve feet of water down there, up against the wharf.'

'Do you mean he's dead?'

'Yes, he's dead.'

It was the first time he had admitted to himself properly, and he felt a great release of the spirit as he did so. There was nothing more he could do for his dory mate.

In the home of one of the seven families in the settlement, the frost was drawn out of Blackburn's hands and feet, after which a poultice was applied and the affected parts bound up. When the bandages were taken off next morning, one finger came away with them. So, in the next few weeks, did all the others, right down to the knuckles. So too did all his toes.

But incredibly enough, the sea adventures of Howard Blackburn had hardly begun. New skin grew over his severed knuckles and they healed well, and he subsequently made two lone crossings of the Atlantic. In 1899 he sailed across in a 30-foot sloop, completing the voyage from Gloucester Massachusetts to Gloucester England in 62 days. And in 1901 he crossed in another sloop, a 25-footer of his own design and construction, arriving safely in Lisbon after 39 days at sea. This time he was not entirely alone; his companion was a fox terrier. When he finally finished with the sea the people of Gloucester took up a subscription for him and set him up in business in a small bar and saloon in the town, and he ran this business until shortly before his death in 1932 at the age of 74.

* * *

Mrs. Isabel F. Hill, reference librarian of the Sawyer Free Library at Gloucester, Massachusetts, kindly sent me the account of Howard Blackburn's ordeal on which my story is based. The original account was written largely in Blackburn's own words following an interview with him not long before his death. 'Mr. Blackburn's story is one our most choice,' wrote Mrs. Hill. 'We tell it to our school children every year when they visit the Library for a historical talk.'

'Captains Courageous', the award-winning film of the Thirties (recently revived on TV), also tells the story of the hazardous life of the dory fishermen.

10

The Man who Fell Overboard

The 'graveyard' watch on the 5,800-ton freighter *British Monarch*—midnight to four o'clock—was nearing its end. Pacing back and forth in the bridge housing, his night vision fully acclimatised after his four-hour vigil, the officer of the watch, 23-year-old Douglas Wardrop, peered into the unrelieved blackness of the Pacific night. There was no horizon, but the stars provided a canopy, and he could just make out the undulating surface of the sea.

These were the hours when the body's metabolism was at its lowest, when even the ship seemed inclined to slumber. Gone was the noise, bustle and activity of the day. Of the 40 crew, only the helmsman, narrow-eyed at the wheel, and the look-out, a shadowy figure on the starboard wing of the bridge, were on watch. The rest were asleep in their bunks. All that disturbed the silence was the monotonous pulsation of the diesel engines, relieved by the intermittent clicking of the wheel under the helmsman's pressure and the incongruous rattling of a cup on a tray.

Punctually at four o'clock the mate, Joe Love, arrived on the bridge. Helmsman and look-out, too, were about to change over.

'Good morning, Mr. Love. It's a wonderful night. We're on a course of 278 degrees. There's no ship in sight—we've seen nothing for hours. Everything's shipshape except the log repeater in the chart room, which isn't working. I'll fix it. Good night, Mr. Love.'

'Good night, Douggie.'

Wardrop left the bridge and automatically headed for his cabin. He was longing for sleep. Then he remembered that he had to correct the fault in the log repeater. If he did it now he could have a lie-in in the morning. He didn't want to be called out too early. With his torch to light the way he directed his steps astern.

He was wearing only a singlet and shorts, but even on the open deck the night air struck deliciously warm. The bracket that held the log clock extended two feet over the stern on the starboard side. He climbed up on to the flat surface of the taffrail and examined the clock face.

As he expected, the log line, trailing 120 feet astern with a spinner on the end, was correctly recording the distance run on the clock face. The trouble must lie in the electrical connection to the repeater. It was a common enough fault. The terminals that made the connection got salted-up. With his torch in his left hand he began to unscrew the clock face to clean the terminals with his right, steadying himself on the bracket with the hand that held the torch.

It was an action that he had performed many times, both during his apprenticeship and in his years as third and now second mate. He had forgotten that he was doing something inherently dangerous, that he should have made quite sure they were watching him from the bridge. He was tired, and the ship was lurching on the swell. Suddenly he felt his grip on the bracket loosening.

For a moment, in the darkness, he was unconscious of the danger. Then he panicked. Clawing with both hands, scrabbling with his feet, he fought desperately to hold on. But the log bracket was fractionally beyond his outstretched fingers. His weight had tipped over too far for recovery, and with a shocked astonishment that was tempered by sheer incredulity he found himself falling—tumbling past the stern with arms flailing and legs outflung.

He hit the water with flat, walloping impact, sending up an explosive splash that someone must surely hear. But it was lost in the churning of the propeller. It must be some hideous nightmare—but it was all too real.

The log line! He had to catch hold of the log line. That was his only hope. If he could hang on to that he could somehow attract attention. Then they would haul him back on board. Could he reach it? He had fallen directly under the bracket, and the line must be immediately above him. As he came up he saw it and grasped it. For the moment he was safe.

The glow of the white stern light threw eerie shadows in which he could just discern the outline of the superstructure. But the 25 feet he had fallen from taffrail to water towered above him now like a beetling precipice. He would never get back without help.

Sixty feet in front of him he could see the lights in the portholes of the poop, reflected from the central light in the mess room. The crew lived aft, and he began shouting for help. There were at least six men within thirty feet of him, he knew. They would be asleep, but someone would hear him.

The ship was making 10 to 12 knots, and being dragged through the water at that speed was giving him a pounding. He had little breath left to shout. The crew accommodation was right above the propeller, and the steering gear, with its continual noise, was in the same area. His shouts became more feeble as he realised no one could hear.

He waved his torch despairingly. What was the use? He wouldn't be able to hold on much longer. Instead of planing along on the surface, as he had hoped, he was being dragged through the swell, half-choked by every fresh wave. The buffeting was forcing the air out of his lungs as soon as he breathed it. It was almost like being dragged at speed over rough ground.

The manilla rope of the log line was cutting into his hands. It would be many hours before they would miss him, yet he couldn't take much more of this.

He hung on grimly now, knowing his life depended on it. But his hands were slipping on the rope, burning his fingers and palms. The pain was excruciating, but he must not let go. Suddenly the pain eased. He looked up—and the stern of the ship was receding. It couldn't be! Without realising it, he had let go.

One last feeble, tortured shout, and he abandoned himself to bleak, undiluted despair. There was no hope for him now—no hope whatever. It would be many hours before they missed him, and long before then he would drown.

The stern of the ship loomed in sombre outline against the night sky, mocking his anguish. Soon all he could see was the stern light. Then even that was gone, and he was utterly alone.

As second mate he knew the hopelessness of his situation all too well; the reaction of wretchedness and desolation was overwhelming. Four days out from Panama, bound for Japan, they were far out in the Pacific, a thousand miles from the nearest land. They had not seen a ship for many hours. There was no chance for him unless the *British Monarch* turned back—and little enough even then. How would they find him in this vast infinity of ocean, not even knowing when he fell overboard? He didn't have a chance in hell.

It was pointless swimming after the ship like this. That would only waste his strength. He tried floating, but that was no good; he was continually being swamped by the swell. He began treading water, keeping himself afloat with his arms. How could he have been so foolish? Why hadn't he told Joe Love he was going aft there and then? He winced with the awful bitterness of self-recrimination. He had chucked his life away.

Instinctively he went on treading water. And in his black despondency he found one consolation. The water seemed buoyant. He was keeping afloat easily enough. At least he could last out until daylight. Perhaps they would have come back by then.

But a moment's logical thought dismissed this as a vain

hope. Everyone would imagine he was in his bunk. Joe Love would note that the log repeater was still malfunctioning, but he would assume that his intention had been to fix it in daylight.

He might be missed at breakfast. But it was Sunday morning—Whit Sunday, 9th June, 1957. Sunday on board ship was a rest day. They would think he was having a lie-in. The thought only deepened his gloom.

Yet surely he would be missed on the bridge. Although he wasn't due on watch again until midday, it was his duty to wind and set the chronometer. No one else was allowed to touch it. That duty was scheduled to be carried out between 8 and 8.30, and it had to be noted in the log. If he failed to discharge it, and if the master, Captain Coutts, was aware of it, he would be on his tail. There was hope there.

But would he notice it? Would anybody tell him? And wouldn't it be too late anyway? He would have been in the water $4\frac{1}{2}$ hours by then. He doubted if he could last that long. And it would still take them another $4\frac{1}{2}$ hours to steam back.

He tried to picture the scene on the ship. It tranquillised his imagination, helped to ease his agony of mind. Sooner or later they must discover that he was missing. Joe Love, the last man to see him, would relate the incident of his promise to repair the log repeater, and they would reach the obvious conclusion. What would they do then?

Captain Coutts would turn back. Of course he would. Never for an instant could he allow himself to doubt that. He had to believe it, to preserve his sanity.

52-year-old William Coutts, a dour Shetlander, was one of the old school. A typical sea-dog of his generation, he didn't take easily to youngsters. But Wardrop trusted him. Captain Coutts would do all he could to find him. All, that is, that was reasonable. Wardrop closed his mind to any deeper analysis.

He escaped again into vivid imaginings of what must be

happening on board. His watch had stopped, but he could tell that dawn was near from the growing pallor of the night sky. It must be about 5.30. The horizon was beginning to sharpen, and he pictured Joe Love going out on to the wing of the bridge to take his morning star-shots. He had done it so often himself. Make it good, Joe Love, for God's sake make it good. Make it spot on. You're going to need the most accurate fix of your life when you find out what's happened.

Daylight brought renewed hope. It also brought palpable evidence of the vast, empty void of the Pacific. He turned wistfully towards Panama to watch the sunrise. It could so easily be the last one he'd see.

He was beginning to have the welcome diversion of company. First it was the birds, small brown creatures with long beaks and eagle eyes. They hovered around briefly, and only one of them stayed for long, dive-bombing him several times to get a closer look, more inquisitive, or perhaps hungrier, than the rest. Hungrier. That was when he remembered the sharks.

Mercifully, he had forgotten them so far. But these were shark-infested waters—killer sharks, and barracuda too. He ducked under the surface to see what might be lurking beneath him, and deep in the pale blue water he saw a sleek, shadowy, oblong shape, furtive and menacing. It was a shark.

A hungry shark would have a go at him, and if that happened, well, that would be the end. He prayed that it might be quick. He was still wearing light-weight shoes, and he determined to kick out all the time, using his shoes for protection. The disturbance he created frightened the shark away.

He felt a stinging sensation in his neck and shoulders, and lifting an arm he saw that something transparent was wrapped around it. He was caught in a shoal of electric eels, and they were writhing all over his body, their pale blue suckers stinging him painfully. Clawing them off, he thrashed and beat at them until they desisted and the shoal moved on.

He tried to forget his body and let his mind wander. He was back at his preparatory school at Seaford, and his father, a local doctor, was still alive. He had been 5½ when his father was killed in Crete. Evacuated to a farm in Warwickshire, he had never heard a bomb drop. Suddenly his father seemed close again. 'Come on, Doug, keep it up, you can do it.'

All seamen, he thought, were a bit religious, though they'd probably tell you they weren't. It was difficult not to be, working so close to the elements. He remembered his first voyage in the China Sea, when they had been hit by a typhoon and no one had thought they could survive. The lifeboats were splintered, the woodwork round the bridge was smashed, tons of water poured into the engine room, and the accommodation was flooded. In his inexperience he had been thrilled by the violence of it—he hadn't appreciated the danger. He had gone into the chart room—and there was the captain, down on his knees. 'If you've got any sense, boy,' he had said, 'you'll pray as well.'

Always his imagination worked back to the ship, and to what was happening on board. Captain Coutts would come up from his cabin about seven o'clock. He would step into the chart room, measure off the distance run, and have a look at the weather reports. Then he would emerge on to the bridge. 'Good morning, Mr. Love—it's going to be a good day.' He would sniff the air and get the feel of the ship. Then at eight o'clock he would appear in the ward room for breakfast.

But before that, at 7.45, Wardrop's steward would knock on the door of his cabin. Getting no answer, he would go in. He would see that the bed had been slept in—Wardrop had rested before going on watch at midnight and he hadn't made the bed—and he would imagine that Wardrop was having a shower. He would put a cup of tea on his bedside locker and leave.

Wardrop saw all this happening as though in a film. It was torture to watch.

Now it was eight o'clock, and one by one the ship's officers were appearing in the ward room for breakfast. Where was the second mate? He had had the graveyard watch, hadn't he? Probably sleeping it off. Oh, he could hear them saying it. But at 8.30, with the captain back on the bridge, and the chronometer not wound—surely they would miss him then? Yet suppose someone, to do him a good turn, wound the chronometer for him? Why hadn't he thought of that?

He had built up so much on that omission, and on the likelihood of the captain noticing it. Now his frail edifice of hope crumbled, and he was wracked again by despair.

It was then that he thought of McNally. Stan McNally was the radio officer, same age as himself. They got on well together, plenty of light-hearted banter. Stan would be looking out for him at breakfast. Surely Stan would miss him.

The notion hardened into certainty, and he clutched at it gratefully, hope returning. He was still managing to keep afloat all right. It would all depend on Stan.

Things were happening on the *British Monarch* very much as Wardrop was imagining them. Even his timing, estimated solely from the height of the sun, was not so very far out.

The steward had taken him his morning tea. There was nothing overtly sinister about the empty cabin. And only one man seemed put out by Wardrop's absence at breakfast. Stan McNally.

'What's the matter with him now?' thought McNally. Wardrop was normally fond of his food. But hadn't he been thinking of dieting? He was certainly a bit overweight. That would explain it.

When he finished his breakfast, McNally went along to Wardrop's cabin to pull his leg. To him, closer to Wardrop than the others, there was something strange about the empty bed, the morning tea left unsampled. It wasn't like Wardrop at all.

Probably he was on the bridge, taking sights. He was nearly always up there somewhere, on duty or no. He went up to the bridge and spoke to the third mate, a young man named Taylor.

'Where's Douggie?'

'Haven't seen him.'

'Where is he, do you think?'

'The mate said something about having trouble with the log during the night. The repeater's not working. Perhaps he's gone down there to fix it.'

So far no one had remarked on the unwound chronometer. Until someone checked the ship's log it wouldn't be noticed.

Stan McNally had his explanation. Why should he look further? But some premonition made him persist. He went aft, and there was no sign of Wardrop. He tried the engine room. He even tried the hold. Back he went to the bridge. 'You'd better tell the captain,' he advised Taylor.

The captain would tell them not to be daft. '*You* tell him.'

McNally did. Captain Coutts bawled him out—but the ship was searched from stem to stern. Wardrop couldn't be found. He had last been seen at four o'clock by the mate. It was now 8.30. Very probably he had been gone for $4\frac{1}{2}$ hours. Turning back would cost time and money. What chance was there of finding him?

Even if Wardrop had somehow survived the sharks and the exposure and remained afloat until now, the chances of his hanging on for twice that time must be remote. His morale would wilt, and that alone would be enough to kill him. Retracing the ship's course precisely, and sighting a tiny dot in the ocean whose position was unknown, were both wildly improbable propositions. Yet as a skilled navigator of long experience Captain Coutts could not stomach the word impossible. He had confidence in the mate, and in his helmsman. He could not bring himself to abandon any member of his crew, let alone a young man as fit and strong as Wardrop, with all the stamina of youth. He would turn round and steer a reciprocal course.

He was asking his crew to perform a miracle. But the decision was made. He believed the owners would back him up.

The vessel had been setting slightly to southward on the way out from Panama. 'If we steer one degree to northward of our true track,' decided Coutts, after consultation with Love, 'we might have a chance of picking him up.' He passed a message to McNally to warn all ships in the area, and signalled the Coastguard at Acapulco for an air search. (But there were no aircraft available.) Then he began laying the new course on the chart.

It's lucky I'm a navigator, thought Wardrop. Had I been a deck hand, or a steward, I'm sure I'd have given up by now. I wouldn't have given myself a chance. But as a navigator I've a right to believe in miracles. I've seen them happen. Even though it's a chance in a million, at least I know roughly when and where to expect the ship, and I'm going to stay afloat if I can, just in case.

That was his resolve. But as the hours passed and he tired of keeping himself afloat, despondency returned. He could see so little from sea level. And visibility would be limited from the deck of the ship—even from the cross-trees and the monkey island, where Captain Coutts would certainly have sited some of the crew.

Suddenly there was a terrific snort behind him, and he wheeled round to see a monstrous head lifting out of the water and blinking huge robot eyes at him. The creature looked almost prehistoric—and then he recognised it as a turtle. What did he know about turtles? This one was a giant specimen, bigger than he was, with eyelids like metal shutters. The creature took one look at him and dived underneath him. He ducked in alarm, but it was swimming gently underneath him, and it came up on the other side, not more than eight feet away.

It's not going to hurt me, thought Wardrop. It didn't appear to have any teeth. It flapped around him, ducking down every so often and making the belching exhalation which had first surprised him. He began to gain confidence.

'Are we going to be friends?' Only now did he realise the intense loneliness of the past few hours. He talked to the turtle continually, explained his problems, told him jokes, sang him songs, described what was happening on the ship. 'They're coming to look for me.' He kept telling himself that. 'They won't be long now.'

Perhaps, with the sun approaching its zenith, he was getting light-headed. He didn't think so. The solitude had been getting him down. The turtle offered the companionship he craved.

The water temperature was about 80 degrees, the air temperature ten to fifteen degrees hotter. He splashed his face to ease the sunburn, but his head and shoulders were blackened and raw.

He was holding on to a rail of some kind now—the rail of a hitching post, it seemed, the sort of thing he had seen in Western films. He didn't know how the post had got there, a thousand miles out in the ocean, but he leaned on it gratefully. All he knew was that he had to hold on until the ship came.

A long time seemed to pass, yet his mind was a blank and

he could remember nothing. He was swimming around again, feeling wonderfully refreshed. He must have fallen asleep, for fully half an hour, judging by the sun. The thought scared him. What had he been holding on to? The hitching post had gone.

The turtle, though, was still there, closer than ever. Could he have been holding on to the turtle? Or had he, in a half-conscious state, imagined the whole thing? No, it could only have been the turtle. This docile creature had saved his life.

His vision was blurred by the constant immersion in salt water, and the colours of sun, sea and sky had merged and run. Yet he still knew the time. It was well after one o'clock. Another few minutes and he would know his fate.

On the bridge of the *British Monarch,* Captain Coutts had an unenviable decision to make. He had run his full distance and seen nothing. Perhaps it had been a forlorn hope anyway. He began to circle. He would give it until 1.30. The time was 1.15.

1.20 came, and then 1.25. There was still no sign of Wardrop. 1.26. 1.27. Three minutes to go.

In the water, Wardrop was thinking of the unpredictable set of the tides and currents in the Pacific. Even the ship's turning circle could put them far enough out to miss him. Suddenly he saw his chances in all their threadbare poverty. He had never really had a chance at all. It was then that he saw the masts.

It was a ship all right, not a mirage. He was sure of that. But the masts were not in line. That puzzled him. It meant that the ship wasn't steaming towards him. Something had gone wrong. And the longer he looked the wider the gap between the masts became. The vessel was turning.

He could just make out a group of tiny figures in the monkey island. Then he saw them in the cross trees and lining the rails. They were all looking for him. But what was this? The ship was turning away. The masts were closing together again. They were giving up and going back. It was the bitterest irony imaginable, the one event he had not foreseen.

Taylor. The third mate. A Perthshire boy. 'Mac' Taylor. He had the sharpest eyesight. Taylor would see him. He *must* see him. He willed it. He lay on his back and splashed in prodigal frenzy, dissipating the last of his strength. It was no further use to him now. The turtle, thoroughly alarmed, made off.

Now, on the bridge, Captain Coutts was blowing the ship's whistle. They had seen him! They were signalling to him! That was what it must mean.

Wardrop's instinct had been right. Taylor, up in the monkey island with a pair of binoculars, had been the one to spot him.

They sent a boat to pick him up, but he insisted on climbing the ladder on his own. Then he collapsed. After nearly $9\frac{1}{2}$ hours in the water he was still wearing his shoes.

$$* \quad * \quad *$$

In 1965, soon after getting married, Douglas Wardrop took a shore job with an insurance company. And today, 15 years after the fantastic piece of navigation—Captain Coutts called it at least 25 per cent luck—that saved his life, he is much the same cheery, youthful, slightly chubby figure as he was then. But there's one delicacy that's off the Wardrop menu for good. Turtle soup.

The Daisy

James Bruce, captain of the Peterhead drifter *Daisy*, heard the mate's voice carry to him in the wheelhouse above the roar and buffeting of the gale. 'We've sprung a leak, skipper. The hold's full of water and the engine's half waterlogged. We've got the pumps going but the water's still rising.'

It was Saturday lunch-time, 4th August, 1962. After a fortnight's drift-net fishing for herring further north they were 40 miles off the Orkneys on a southerly course, heading for Peterhead and home. Their catch had been poor, and they had stayed an extra day in the fishing grounds to try to haul another few cran. Otherwise they would have been where most of the other Peterhead boats were right now—safe in the shelter of their home port on the Aberdeenshire coast, a week-end's rest ahead of them.

'I'll come and have a look.'

Handing over the wheel, Bruce hurried amidships and climbed down the hatch into the engine-room. The base of the engine was submerged, and as Andrew Reid, the mate, had said, the pumps were losing ground.

The *Daisy* was a new 50-ton drifter, only eighteen months old, launched in March of the previous year. 76 feet long, she was fully equipped with all modern fittings and safety devices. What could have gone wrong?

Bruce hurried back to the wheelhouse. First he eased back the throttles, reducing his speed from six knots to three. At once the stem of the vessel dipped and the stern came up. The volume of water she was taking forward had already unbalanced her. She might go down within minutes.

As Bruce grabbed the telephone-type transmitter/receiver behind him to put out a distress call he looked at the ship's clock. Right now the weather forecast for shipping was being broadcast: every vessel in the area would be tuned in to the B.B.C. Until that forecast was through there was no chance of getting an answer on the trawler wave-band.

The tilt of the ship was getting even more pronounced. 'Get the rafts ready, Andrew,' he called to the mate. 'And keep those pumps going. See if you can hold her. I'll have to wait for the forecast—that means another five minutes.'

Only a few hours earlier, when they had turned from the Bressay fishing grounds for home, their Decca navigator had packed up. That hadn't mattered so long as they were bound for Peterhead. But now, just when giving their exact position might be a vital factor in getting assistance, they would be unable to do so.

Other unpleasant thoughts were crowding into Bruce's mind. On a Saturday afternoon, the few trawlers that might be in the area would be, like themselves, homeward bound. No one fished on a Sunday. In spite of the fierceness of the storm there would be an air of relaxation on board. When the shipping forecast was over most of the crews would stay tuned to the B.B.C. They wouldn't switch to the trawler wave-band except to pass some routine message. By that time it might be too late for the *Daisy*.

James Bruce, 26, was the youngest of the three Bruce brothers who owned the *Daisy*. All were on board. James was captain because as a bachelor he had been the only one who could afford to give the time to taking his ticket. But there was more to it than that. Good-humoured and imperturbable, he soon earned the respect of his crew and became the acknowledged leader. There was no jealousy from the elder brothers; each was one of the team. All had been to sea since boyhood; their father had been a trawler skipper. His ship, too, had been called the *Daisy*.

All the crew were young men, fit and strong, solid as the red granite, quarried nearby, of which their town was built. Andrew Bruce was the oldest at 31. Youngest was Bruce

Strachan, whose job it was to coil the ropes. Every young fellow started like that. His mother had tried hard to dissuade him from going to sea, but it had been no use. He was 15.

When at last the shipping forecast was over, James Bruce began his call on the trawler wave-band. 'Mayday, Mayday, Mayday. *Daisy* calling any ships in the vicinity. We are making water fast and require assistance.'

He took his finger off the transmitter button and waited. Surely someone would hear them. Then a voice crackled in his ear loud and clear.

'*Fairweather* calling *Daisy*. Your message received. What is your position?'

'We've no Decca, it's broken down. But we shot our nets last night two hours south-east of Lerwick. We've been steering for Peterhead from that position for ten hours at 7 knots.'

Bruce had no time to work out the position himself; he would have to leave that to the *Fairweather*. Looking back from the wheelhouse he saw that both the life-rafts were out of their containers and inflated on deck. Then he repeated his Mayday call so that other ships could take a bearing on him.

'Do you require air assistance?' asked the captain of *Fairweather*.

'Yes please.'

The stem of the *Daisy* was now under water—the sea was flooding over the deck. Bruce shouted back to Reid. 'Launch the life-rafts. We're abandoning ship.' And he made a final call on the radio. 'Mayday, Mayday, we're sinking fast. I'll transmit again for you to get bearings. We are getting in the rafts now. We are all in good heart. Any vessel in the vicinity, please make for us at full speed. I'm leaving now.'

The rest of the crew had got into the rafts, five in one and four in the other. The rafts were, in fact, large rubber dinghies, and there was plenty of room. But the *Daisy* was so

nose-heavy that the stern was now clear of the water, revealing her screws. As a mountainous sea broke over the ship,
one of the dinghies was hurled against the stern, fouling the
screws. They all crowded into the other dinghy, cut the
trapped dinghy adrift, and began paddling clear of the
wreck.

In those final minutes as they prepared to leave the *Daisy*
they had fired several rockets but had seen no other shipping. Visibility in the gale was down to one mile, however,
and several other ships might be quite close to them. They
had got their distress call out, and they had given a rough
position. It could not be long before they were picked up.

Their immediate concern was to get clear of the *Daisy*
before another mountainous sea drove them back towards the
screws, and they paddled strenuously. The dinghy seemed
strong and seaworthy, tightly inflated, and above them a
canopy protected them completely. There was a flap at
either end for access and for keeping a look-out, and a tiny
glow from a light in the roof. They would be safe in here for
a time.

That was how it seemed. But they had paddled no more
than fifty yards when Reid shouted a warning. 'Watch your-
selves, lads—lump of water!' That was all he had time to say
before a towering mass of sea hit them broadside on, throwing everyone to the far side of the dinghy. Thus unbalanced
the dinghy was easily tossed up and over. Two men were
thrown out as it somersaulted, and the rest were trapped
underneath. They found themselves standing on the roof,
with the bottom of the dinghy above their heads and the
water in the dinghy up to their chests. There was just
sufficient trapped air for them to breathe.

Unless they could right the dinghy they were finished.
And two men were struggling outside. Crawling through the
submerged entrance flap, James Bruce escaped into the sea
and climbed on top of the capsized dinghy. He was joined at
once by Andrew Reid and James Thain, the two men who

had been thrown out, and they started to try to pull the dinghy over. Realising what was going on, the men inside helped by pushing to one side, and the dinghy was successfully righted.

Soaked and momentarily exhausted, they set to work at once to bale out the swamped dinghy. There was only one baler, and they used their shoes.

They hadn't properly realised the danger they were in until now. Tempestuous seas and gale force winds threatened to capsize the dinghy again and again. How long would they withstand such a buffeting? However much they tried to reassure themselves, the fact remained that their precise position was unknown. Other vessels might be near, but none had seen their visual signals. They had abandoned one dinghy, and been thrown out once of the other. They had lost some of their supplies, and worse still, all but six of their handflares. In this heaving sea, drifting before the gale, the dinghy would be hard to find.

The first need, thought Bruce, was for some method of strengthening and steadying the dinghy. The weight of their bodies would help if properly distributed, and he set to work to adjust the trim, arranging the men on either side, getting the men on one side to push hard with their feet against the knees of the men opposite. The effect was of a series of rigid supports across the diameter of the dinghy, helping them to hold their position and prevent a sudden shift of weight to one side in plunging seas. They also released the drogue, a canvas sea anchor which helped to steady the dinghy and reduce their rate of drift.

James Bruce and Reid took up position beside the escape flaps at either end. As the strongest swimmers they were the best equipped to take action if the dinghy capsized again.

The *Fairweather*, which was too far away to help, had passed the *Daisy*'s distress call on to the nearest shore station by radio, and the trawler *Westward*, after taking D/F bearings on Bruce's transmissions, had sent out a position of

58.53 North, 01.15 West, roughly 60 miles east and slightly south of Kirkwall. Such a bearing was not likely to be more than approximate, but it gave something to go on, and several ships were already hurrying towards the position.

The Coastguard Station at Wick, and the Northern Rescue Co-ordination Centre at Pitreavie Castle, had both been alerted by radio messages. The Stronsay lifeboat, from the island of Stronsay, 40 miles distant, was advised to launch, and the R.A.F. were putting up a Shackleton from Ballykelly, Northern Ireland. Both were on their way to the estimated position of the sinking within half an hour. By that time the *Westward* was already in the search area, looking for the *Daisy*'s crew. A Force 8 gale was blowing and visibility was bad in rainstorms and mist, but ten other vessels of various nationalities were approaching the area and some were already in company with the *Westward*. Nothing was seen.

The Shackleton, piloted by Flight Lieutenant Roger Britton, reached the search area about four o'clock, two hours after the *Daisy* went down. Broadcasts from the shore stations at Stonehaven and Wick were now giving a revised position for the life-rafts—it was thought there were two—to take account of drift. With a drogue out it was not thought that drift would exceed two to three knots. The direction of the drift was to the north-east, away from the islands.

Other trawlers in the area, German, Danish and Norwegian, were hauling in their nets and joining the search. The German fisher-cruiser *Anton Dohrn* reported that it was 26 miles from the estimated position of the sinking and was organising its fleet of trawlers to cover the entire area. Hour by hour the shore stations transmitted an amended position of the life-rafts to allow for drift. By six o'clock the Stronsay lifeboat was only 25 miles from the latest computed position.

Flight Lieutenant Britton and his crew, hampered by low cloud and driving rain, peering down at a surging, switchback sea, were covering the area systematically from 200 feet. After two hours of fruitless searching they made their first sighting—a red and white lifebelt, a yellow door, and a fish-box. This must surely be wreckage thrown up by the *Daisy*.

Britton's navigator plotted the new position as 12 miles east of the position estimated by the *Westward*, on which the search had so far been based. His crew marked the wreckage with a smoke float. The new position was given to the Rescue Centre and at once broadcast to all concerned. A new search area was designated, centred on a point several miles downwind of the wreckage.

Every vessel in the area was converging on a position that seemed to have been computed with convincing accuracy; the finding of the wreckage had removed the element of uncertainty, and a sighting seemed imminent. But at 6.45 that evening, when the Buckie trawler *Amethyst* passed alongside the smoke float dropped by the Shackleton, the crew could see no sign of wreckage, and the captain reported this on the trawler wave-band. When this news reached Pitreavie Castle they asked the Shackleton to re-establish the position of the wreckage and check the co-ordinates given.

Tracking back towards the smoke float, Flight Lieutenant Britton and his crew confirmed its position. But the wreckage they had seen so clearly 90 minutes earlier had gone. Had they identified it correctly? Had it really come from the *Daisy*? The crew themselves were sure of what they had seen, but the report from the *Amethyst* threw an ominous shadow across the whole arithmetic of the search. Rescue before nightfall, which at first had seemed certain, was now problematical; a crisis in the search operation had been reached. Yet the existing search area remained the most likely one, and it was not changed.

By half-past seven, 15 German trawlers were combing the area under the control of the *Anton Dohrn*, heading northeast on a front 10–12 miles wide. The Shackleton too was

M

overhead again, firing rockets to delineate the limits of the search area and to direct the ships. At eight o'clock the Stronsay lifeboat appeared on the scene and headed north-east. It seemed incredible that this international armada of seaching craft could fail to sight the rafts.

Flight Lieutenant Britton, instructed to carry out a wide sweep before nightfall, brought his Shackleton down to 100 feet and estimated that the waves were 20 feet high. He counted between 30 and 40 ships in the area; it was fright-ening to watch them plunging into the troughs, with the waves towering above them. He doubted whether a dinghy could survive in such a sea.

What chance was there of finding the rafts in darkness? It was known that each dinghy was equipped with flares, so the situation was not hopeless. At half-past eight a policy for a night search was broadcast. The Shackleton would carry out its normal night search technique; meanwhile the ships would spread out over a wide area, and the Shackleton would fire green flares to indicate turning points.

A crowd had gathered at the harbour at Peterhead, where the crews of over 20 trawlers, most of whom had only just returned from the fishing grounds, were preparing to put to sea again in spite of weather which might normally have deterred them. The decision to sail, when it came, was in-stinctive and unanimous. The sea, their benefactor, was also the common enemy.

There was nothing haphazard about their plans. The *Aurora,* captained by James Watt, an ex-Naval man, would act as link ship to direct the trawlers in a carefully organised search; they expected to reach the search area some time after daylight.

Few of the wives or relatives of the missing men were amongst the growing crowd at the harbour. Most had been sitting by their radios ever since the news of the sinking came through, listening out on the trawler wave-band. The name of another fishing vessel was in everyone's mind, although no one spoke of it. In February of that year the trawler *Ocean Maid,* with six Peterhead men on board, had been caught in the fishing grounds in bad weather and had disappeared without trace.

Towards midnight the Longhope lifeboat, south of Kirkwall, left to relieve the men from Stronsay.[1] And early on the morning of 5th August, 23 trawlers sailed from Peterhead, bringing the total search force to about 60 vessels. Meanwhile the *Anton Dohrn* had reported that the whole search area had been covered since darkness fell; apart from the occasional flare from the circling Shackleton nothing had been seen. At Ballykelly, the crew of a second Shackleton were having an early breakfast prior to taking off to relieve Britton and his crew.

Flight Lieutenant Bill Houldsworth, captain of the second Shackleton, was as mystified as anyone at the lack of success of the search. But at briefing in the Ballykelly operations room he and his navigator, Nigel Read, wondered whether enough drift was being allowed for in the gale that was still blowing. The trouble was that the successive areas of search could not be combed thoroughly before the dinghies were calculated to have drifted out of them. And in Houldsworth's opinion the drift ought to be estimated as a full three knots, probably more. That might explain why the dinghies hadn't been found.

Houldsworth was a practical man and he knew that the main search area had been carefully calculated and that he would be unlikely to get it altered. But he was convinced that the dinghy must be at the north-eastern limit of the search area or beyond. He decided to ask permission to start his

1. The Longhope lifeboat, with its entire crew, was lost seven years later, in 1969.

search at a point say 100 miles north-east of where the *Daisy* crew had abandoned ship—that, he thought, was about the limit of credibility—and spend an hour or so on his own private search before coming back to cover the briefed area. This, at half-past one that morning, was the question he put to the controller at Pitreavie Castle. The controller, perhaps, knew his man: permission to spend one hour on such a search was granted.

Soon after three o'clock the Peterhead trawlers were advised to rendezvous at 59 degrees North, 01 degrees West at 05.30, spread themselves out on an oblique line running north-west to south-east, and then search on a north-east course for 30 miles. Although allowing for the further drift of the raft as the hours passed, this was fundamentally the area covered by the German trawlers during the night; it was still thought to be the most likely area.

On that Sunday morning the drama of the *Daisy* became front-page news. When Houldsworth took off from Ballykelly, Press reporters and TV cameramen were on board his Shackleton. By 4.15 he had taken over from Britton and had reached a point 100 miles downwind of the estimated point of the sinking. He then began a criss-cross search which brought him steadily back towards the official search area. Like Britton he was hampered by rainstorms and poor visibility, but soon after first light the cloud-base lifted and he was able to search from a height of 500 feet.

At 4.52 there was a shout from the crew member at the port beam window; Flight Sergeant Reg Rowe had sighted a rectangular yellow object. He rushed to the flare chute to mark the spot—but the chute jammed. By the time he had cleared it the Shackleton was nearly a mile further on. Rowe dropped a flame float at a distance of one mile, and another at two miles, and then Houldsworth back-tracked over them, fully expecting to see the dinghy a mile beyond the second float. But there was nothing there.

It was the wreckage story all over again. Could Rowe

have been mistaken? He was adamant that he could not. What the object had been was another matter, and like Britton he doubted if anyone could survive in a dinghy in that sea. But he felt sure he had seen something worth investigating.

They were still searching well to the east of the briefed area, purely on a personal hunch. Could they risk diverting the entire searching force to this position on the strength of a sighting they could not confirm? This was the dilemma that faced Houldsworth. For the next 45 minutes he circled the position, until the hour that he had been allowed had stretched into an hour and a quarter and more. He was overdue in the briefed search area and they would have to leave. But Houldsworth, wrestling with his doubts, retained enough confidence in his crew to send a sighting report, belated as it was. 'Yellow object sighted,' he signalled, 'in position 59.10 North 00.03 East. Have tried to relocate without success. Resuming search in briefed area.' The time was 05.35.

Houldsworth's message was re-broadcast to the searching ships and they altered course for the position he gave. The nearest vessels were the *Anton Dohrn*, 25 miles away, and a Danish vessel, the *Nella Dan*, slightly more distant. The Peterhead trawlers were only just forming up. The *Anton Dohrn* gave its estimated time of arrival at the new position as 08.30—a delay of nearly three hours.

Thus while Houldsworth, uncertain what the yellow object was, was taking up the search in the briefed area, the entire seaborne force was hurrying eastwards to the position he had given.

'Are you able to positively identify the object?' That was the question asked of the Rescue Co-ordination Centre. The query was inevitably passed on to Houldsworth, and he answered it cautiously.

'No. It was only an object. We couldn't identify it. But we thought it might give a lead.'

At eleven minutes past eight the *Anton Dohrn* reported sighting a length of rope near the position given by Houldsworth. Yellowed by immersion in the sea, it could conceivably have been the object sighted by Rowe. Then the *Nella Dan* reported in. 'Am in position given, the visibility is 5–7 miles, nothing sighted.' The skipper added that he would search downwind.

The operation had reached a fresh crisis. If the Rowe sighting ended in disillusion, as seemed likely, many hours would have been lost and a fresh approach to the problem would have to be made.

As darkness fell the previous evening, James Bruce had sent up one of his five remaining flares. There was no answering light. Every half-hour since the sinking he had climbed out on the rim of the dinghy and scanned the horizon, but visibility was so limited at sea level that he doubted whether he could see more than a mile. Once or twice they thought they heard aircraft engines, but they never caught so much as a glimpse of a searching plane. Everything was dwarfed and drowned by the roar of the gale and the continual threat of another overwhelming sea.

The measures Bruce and the crew had taken to avoid capsizing had been successful so far. Everything depended on each man holding his position in the dinghy; but they were becoming dangerously cramped and fatigued.

It was warm under the canopy, and even in their wet clothes they did not feel cold. Indeed they had to open the flap periodically to freshen the stale air. For supper they had biscuits, barley sugar and a tiny ration of water. Only one man had a watch, and it had stopped, but they set it to what they guessed the time was and got it going again. From then on Bruce organised them into watches—two men fully alert for each half-hour while the others relaxed as much as they dare. No one slept; the threat from the sea was too great.

They had not had a smoke since the sinking, and when they turned out their pockets just before nightfall they found that only one man had a packet that was not completely saturated. That was the engineer, Alex Sutherland. He had a full packet of twenty. Ten were soaked, ten were dry. Just one each. They lit up from the hand flare they sent up—without effect—at dusk.

Sometimes they prayed silently to themselves, sometimes they sang. Pop songs and hymns alternated without incongruity. As night fell Alex Sutherland said a prayer out loud, and they joined in with him.

They had no idea how far they had drifted, but they were conscious that the rescue operations which they were certain must have been mounted had somehow gone wrong. They had not forgotten the *Ocean Maid*, or the many other vessels that had disappeared at intervals over the years. Yet somehow they kept their confidence in rescue. 'We can't drown,' said the cook, James Cowie, 'I was born with a caul.'

At daybreak Bruce sent up another flare, and he and Andrew Reid scanned the sky for an answer. Again there was nothing. Three flares left. We shan't use another, decided Bruce, until we see a ship or a plane.

On board the *Anton Dohrn* and the *Nella Dan,* and on the many other fishing vessels hurrying to the new position given by Houldsworth, the look-outs had been doubled and the search intensified. Then, soon after half-past eight, James Bruce, leaning through the flap of the dinghy, suddenly shouted to the rest of the crew.

'*It's a great big beauty!*'

Two or three miles away, coming into view intermittently as the dinghy pitched and rolled from the troughs to the wave-tops, was a small red-painted ship which looked as big as a giant tanker to Bruce. Grabbing one of the flares, he released it immediately, barely glancing at it as it curved skywards. He did not take his eyes off the ship.

'They haven't seen us.'

Bruce sent up another flare, and there was still no indication that they had been seen. He had only one flare left, and he fired it.

The two men in the crow's nest of the *Nella Dan*—this was the ship that had come into view—had in fact already seen the raft. In the next moment the ship blew her siren, and the men under the canopy cheered frantically in return. A signal was sent out then by the *Nella Dan*. 'Life-raft found, there are people on board.'

Half an hour later, half-paralysed after 19 hours of bracing every muscle to hold their position in the dinghy, the crew of the *Daisy* were safely aboard the *Nella Dan*. Soon afterwards they were transferred to the Longhope lifeboat and brought back to Scotland.

What caused the sinking of the *Daisy* was never established. She was not the only ship to spring a leak that day—another trawler, the *Honey Bee*, just managed to limp back into port without assistance.

The dinghy had drifted for over 60 miles by the time it was found, keeping just outside the eastern limit of the search area throughout. It is a moot point whether or not the massive surface search would eventually have caught up with it, but Bill Houldsworth's hunch made sure. What really saved the crew, however, was their own resolve and endurance in stabilising the dinghy, preventing a succession of somersaults that would otherwise have exhausted them long before they were found.

* * *

A new *Daisy* was built at a local yard in Peterhead and four of the old crew are now sailing in her. They are the three Bruce brothers, James, Andrew and William George, and the mate Andrew Reid. James Thain is now part owner of the seine netter *Constant Friend*,

Bruce Strachan is a crew member of a successful purse netter, the *Vigilant*, and another crew member, James McLean, is captain of his own seine netter. All the crew remained at sea except the engineer, Alex Sutherland, who joined the local fish canning factory as a fitter; but recently, as engineer in the seine netter *Graceful*, he went back to sea.

The Wreck of the Stella

'I shall be there on time,' said Captain Reeks, the burly, florid master of the London and South Western Railway Company's Channel steamer *Stella*, 'if I break my neck to do it. I mean to get into Guernsey before the G.W.R. boat from Weymouth if I can.'

It was the Easter holiday excursion, the first daylight express of the season, the Thursday before Good Friday, 30th March 1899. They were exciting times. The 19th Century was going out with a bang. Barnum and Bailey were at Olympia with the greatest show on earth. The Belle of New York, with full American company, was at the Shaftesbury, Ada Reeve was topping the bill at the Palace. A young man named Marconi was experimenting with cross-Channel wireless communication. 21,000 British subjects in the Transvaal, their grievances ignored by Kruger and his government, were petitioning the Queen.

Queen Victoria herself was spending Easter at Nice. The Prince of Wales, soon to become Edward VII, was at Cannes.

These were the days of hectic rivalry between the big railway companies. The London and South Western's holiday excursion to Guernsey and Jersey left Waterloo that morning at 8.55. The train went to the quayside at Southampton, where passengers transferred to the *Stella*, 1,059 tons and a top speed of 18½ knots. Arrival at Guernsey was timed for 5.30.

The Great Western's holiday excursion to the Channel Islands left Paddington five minutes earlier, at 8.50. Passengers were taken to the quayside at Weymouth and embarked on the *Ibex*, 1,151 tons and a top speed of 19 knots. Arrival at Guernsey was timed for—5.30.

Given clear weather, the last hour of the voyage would be a thrilling one as the two ships sighted each other and strove to head each other off before entering the Little Russel, the narrow channel between the rocks off Guernsey. There would be many wagers and much tipping and urging of firemen on both boats.

Puffs for the two services competed side by side in the newspaper advertisement columns. The South Western service was the 'shortest and best'. The Great Western countered with the 'quickest and best'. They had some justification for the billing. Complaints of the late arrival of the *Stella* and her sister-ships had been frequent, and the Jersey Chamber of Commerce had recently commented on their chronic unpunctuality as compared with the boats of the G.W.R.

In his double-breasted pilot coat with brass buttons, its severity relieved by the two gold rings on the cuff of the sleeve, the solid, strongly-built Captain Reeks was a commanding figure. One of the passengers, Edgar Anderson, a painter, noted the clean-shaven, vivid complexion, varied only by a sandy, unruly moustache, and dominated by a prominent nose and bright, blue-grey eyes. The man would be a good subject for a portrait.

In the mind of Captain Reeks there was a single, niggling worry. His normal good temper had been severely tested by the newspaper reports criticising the South Western service, and he had been particularly upset by one article complaining that on a recent Saturday his ship had been 12 hours late. A man who navigated across the Atlantic in bad weather could be four days late and still be a hero. The hazards of the Channel crossing were considerable, but to be late was to be jeered at—especially if the rival service had beaten you to it.

The management would protest that they would never countenance racing; but pressure was implicit in the timing of the two services. The *Stella* was competing for traffic on a lightly-used route with a great rival company, and the Easter daylight excursion was a prestige venture. That was why Captain Reeks was determined to be on time.

The *Stella* got under way at 11.27, twelve minutes late, and steamed off down the Solent carrying about 150 passengers and 40 crew. (Detailed passenger lists were not kept.) She was a trim, neat vessel, schooner-rigged, with a yellow funnel, built on the Clydebank in 1890. She had just been overhauled and repainted, and her white superstructure stood out clearly, topped by the bridge and the boat deck, where four boats were stowed inboard on davits—a lifeboat and a cutter on each side. A fifth boat—a dinghy—was suspended above the quarter-deck to starboard. Below the boat deck was the promenade deck, then the main deck and gangways. Today the long, low outline forward of the superstructure was broken by the external stowage of a 2-ton pantechnicon van.

Past the Folly Beacon, past the Spit Beacon, down the Leap, and all the way to a point opposite Hurst Castle on the mainland, Captain Reeks was checking his engine revolutions and establishing his speed and position. At 12.44 the *Stella* was off The Needles, the south-western tip of the Isle of Wight. A last position check and Captain Reeks shaped an oblique, south-westerly course for the Casquets, the group of helmet-shaped rocks that lay right across his route 64 miles from The Needles, 17 miles from Guernsey.

It was essential to sight the Casquets in order to set course correctly for the Little Russel and avoid the rocks and islands that littered the approaches to Guernsey. Even in thick fog it was necessary to pass close enough to the Casquets to hear the fog siren on the lighthouse and set course from there.

Captain Reeks had no radio; wireless telegraphy had only just been invented. Radar was unheard of. He would steer for the Casquets by dead reckoning, allowing for the tide, aiming to pass $1\frac{1}{2}$ miles to the west of Black Rock, the western extremity. It was a beautiful Spring day, the wind was light south-westerly, and they would see the Casquets at a distance of ten to fifteen miles and alter course as necessary.

There was a strong swell off The Needles and some of the passengers went to the cabins to lie down. The two stewardesses, Mary Rogers and Ada Preston, were kept busy in the ladies' cabin and saloon. Both came from Southampton, both had gone to sea to augment the family income. Mary Rogers' husband had been lost overboard near the Casquets; she was keeping an aged father, a daughter who stayed at home to look after him, and an apprentice son who earned six shillings a week. Ada Preston was deputising for the regular stewardess, who was ill. It was her first time at sea.

Under the care of the two stewardesses, and of the stewards, most of the seasick passengers relaxed and dozed. Some of the less affected gave instructions to be roused before the ship reached Guernsey. 'Call me when we're off the Casquets,' was a popular request.

Most of the passengers were Londoners who had travelled down by the morning train. Thomas Allen, a tailor in Mark Lane, was travelling with his wife. He was a Dickensian figure, beyond middle age, stout and heavily built, with white hair and full, billowing beard. He and his wife knew Captain Reeks from an earlier voyage. After an early lunch, Allen was enjoying a cigar in the smoking-room when Captain Reeks walked in.

'Are you all comfortable, gentlemen?'

Captain Reeks recognised Allen and walked across to greet him.

'Have you had lunch?'

'Yes.'

'Come and have a drink.'

After they had had a whisky and soda together, Captain Reeks offered Allen and his wife the use of his cabin for the voyage. They accepted gratefully. Then the captain was called to lunch.

Lunch at the captain's table in the dining saloon was a gay affair, dominated by the jocular, affable personality of Captain Reeks. Sharing his table were Edward Abinger, a barrister; the Reverend and Mrs. C. R. Bailey; the tall, regal Mrs. Aylett, dark hair piled on top of her head; and her friend Dr. Philip Davis, analyst, author and journalist. The only disturbing element at lunch was the erratic behaviour of the crockery, which tipped and rattled and shook under the influence of the high engine vibration. The *Stella* was steaming at full speed.

During lunch there was a change in the weather. The sun disappeared behind a bank of cloud, the blue of the sea changed to a leaden grey, the swell vanished, the sea ironed itself out into a flat calm. Soon the air became hazy, visibility deteriorated, and they began to run through patches of fog.

'Isn't it dangerous', Mrs. Aylett asked the captain, 'to run at this speed through fog?'

'The man on the bridge', said Captain Reeks, 'can find his way anywhere.' Reeks was referring to his first officer, a man named Wade, short and well-knit, with dark hair and close-cropped beard, who was in line for promotion to captain. Wade's wife Lillian had come along for the trip.

Shortly after two o'clock, when the *Stella* ran into the thickest fog yet, speed was reduced for a time. But soon the fog gave way to haze, visibility increased to about a mile, and full speed ahead was again the order from the bridge.

Many of the passengers expressed surprise at the high speed that was being maintained. Alderman John Collier, a former mayor of Godalming, stout and sixtyish, was travelling with his son Edward and with Reginald and Ethel Moon, children of a well-known architect and surveyor in Godalming. 'I've been travelling on this course every year for 18 years,' declared Collier, 'and I've never known a vessel driven at such a speed, fog or no fog.' No one demurred. The continuing vibration seemed to support what he said.

Shortly before 3.30 the captain returned to the bridge. On the way he passed Dr. Davis and Mrs. Aylett, who were relaxing on deck. Dr. Davis exchanged a few words with the captain. When he sat down again he spoke to Mrs. Aylett. 'There's no doubt about it,' he said, 'the captain means to get there on time.'

One other passenger spoke to the captain as he made his way to the bridge. Standing near the bridge steps was a man named Colonel George Dixon, a Territorial who was travelling with his wife and son. 'Pity about the fog, Captain,' said Dixon.

'Yes—it threatens to spoil a good run.'

Reeks climbed the steps and took over from Wade, who stayed with him on the bridge. Reeks kept the engines at full speed. He was not due to reach the Casquets for over half an hour. As a warning to other shipping, however, the fog-whistle was sounded at regular intervals—three shrill blasts and then a two-minute break—by a seaman named Davey, who stood on the bridge.

A look-out had been posted right up in the bows on the forecastle head, a hundred feet forward of the bridge. From this vantage point a considerable increase in visibility could be obtained. The name of the look-out was Hartup; but it was his first voyage in the *Stella*. He had little experience of the Channel Islands run and had never seen the Casquets in his life.

The log-line, which recorded the distance run, had been set at The Needles, but it was an inaccurate means of measurement. All the South Western captains preferred to rely on the number of engine revolutions as recorded by their chief engineer.

With an ebb tide the run from The Needles to the Casquets took about 28,000 engine revs. It was Captain Reeks's habit to have a warning from his engine-room at 24,000 revs and again at 26,000. By the time of the third warning he would know that he must be abreast of the Casquets. But in thick fog he would never let his ship run as far as that. His practice was to run to within about three miles of the rocks and then, if he still hadn't heard the fog siren, to slow down and take soundings.

Today the first bell from the engine-room, announcing the completion of 24,000 engine revolutions, came at 3.42. First Officer Wade entered it in the log.

Wade had some business to discuss with the second mate, George Reynolds, about the watch-keeping in port, and he sent for Reynolds to come to the bridge. The time was 3.45. Reynolds was off duty, but the *Stella* was approaching the critical point of her voyage, and after settling his business with Wade he remained on the bridge.

The man at the wheel was an experienced seaman named Johnson, bearded and grizzled, of indeterminate age. He spoke to Captain Reeks. 'The tide's running very slack, sir. Shall I alter course half a point to the west?'

Captain Reeks took a moment to consider. His actual course, without interference from the westerly tide, would take him $5\frac{1}{2}$ miles east of the Casquet lighthouse. But with a seven mile allowance for the tide—the proper allowance—he would pass $1\frac{1}{2}$ miles to the west. It was true that with an abnormally slack tide he might come right on to the Casquets, but he would see them in good time, or hear the fog-horn. If he altered course the danger was that he might miss the Casquets altogether, both by sight and sound, and have no pinpoint to help him find the channel into Guernsey.

'Keep the regular course.'

Reynolds estimated the visibility now as half a mile—just about enough, he thought, to avoid collision with a vessel on an opposite course. The *Stella* was a handy ship—in emergency she could turn completely about in less than half a mile. Captain Reeks kept her at full speed.

At 3.55 the second bell went from the engine room. That meant 26,000 revs. Reynolds made the entry in the log. They were four miles short of the Casquets—a margin of 13 minutes. They began to listen for the fog siren.

Captain Reeks picked up the speaking tube and called the engine room. 'Stand by.' Engineers and firemen, alerted to their posts, stood at the ready, prepared to act instantly on the next order from the bridge.

There was still no swell, but the surface of the sea was crinkled and rippled. Visibility in the vessel's wake was fair, perhaps a mile or more, but abeam it was poor, and it was worst dead ahead.

Passenger Arthur Bush, of Fulham, had got talking to the chief engineer, a Scot from Kilmarnock named Thomas Love, stocky of build, bearded, gentle, very fond of reading and quoting Burns. Love invited Bush to have a look at the engine room, and just before four o'clock Bush went down there. 'We're steaming at $18\frac{1}{2}$ knots,' said Love proudly. Down below they knew nothing of the worsening fog.

Colonel George Dixon went forward and spoke to Hartup, the look-out. 'Oughtn't we to slow down?'

'The captain doesn't think it's thick enough.'

The air was clammy and chill, the wet haze was making the rigging drip unpleasantly, and most of the passengers had left the promenade deck. Some of the men were playing cards in the smoking room. Greta Williams, a well-known contralto of the day, had gone to her cabin with her sister Theresa. Bening and Claude Arnold, aged 14 and 11, tiring of throwing a football to and fro, were playing chess, watched indulgently by their mother. In their Scots kilts and tartans they were a colourful pair.

Bening, the older boy, was studying at the Regent Polytechnic. He had won several medals for swimming.

The bows of the *Stella* still cleaved the grey water at $18\frac{1}{2}$ knots. The fog whistle hooted dismally. The vessel was still steaming full speed ahead through the thick, ghostly haze.

Captain Reeks was confident that he must be comfortably west of the Casquets, even with a slack tide. In any case he still had three miles to go. But if he didn't hear the fog-horn soon he would have to slow down and take soundings. He wondered how the *Ibex* was doing.

Unknown to Captain Reeks the Casquets themselves were completely enveloped in a cocoon of clinging, glutinous fog. The siren at the lighthouse had been hooting all day, but the wind was blowing the sound westwards. Six miles away, on Alderney, it could be heard clearly. But Captain Reeks, now by his own reckoning at less than three miles range, still couldn't hear it.

Reeks knew well enough that sound, especially of sirens, was not to be trusted in thick fog. Large areas of silence were possible, and the foghorn on the Casquets was always fixed into wind and could not be rotated. But today Reeks had not so far encountered anything remotely resembling thick fog. A thick haze, yes; but to a seaman that wasn't fog. He decided to give it another two minutes and then slow down. That was going just about as close as he dared.

The fog-horn on the Casquets was a mechanical one which gave three long blasts in quick succession at intervals of two minutes. Fate decreed that the final two minutes which Captain Reeks allowed himself in which to pick up the Casquets by sight or sound should be the fog-horn's silence period.

The *Stella*'s own fog-whistle was sounding, but it was not heard on the Casquets.

Just before the end of Captain Reeks's two-minute period, with the engineers still standing by for the order to slow down, a single blast of the Casquets' fog-horn was suddenly and clearly heard on board the *Stella*. It sounded incredibly close and seemed to come from almost dead ahead, very slightly on the port bow.

'Port! Hard a-port!'

The shouted order from Captain Reeks came before the hoot of the siren had died away. It was acted on just as quickly by Johnson, the man at the wheel. The order—porting the helm—meant a turn in the reverse direction, a sharp turn to starboard, away from the sound of the siren. But even as the *Stella* swerved violently to the right there came a shout from the look-out man.

'Land dead ahead.'

The rocks of the Casquets were bearing straight down upon them out of the fog, less than a hundred yards away. The *Stella* was still steaming at full speed. She would be on the rocks in ten seconds.

'Full speed astern starboard engine!'

Reynolds, the second mate, standing by the telegraph, backed the starboard engine himself. It would swing the ship round almost at right angles. Down in the engine room, Love and his team of engineers moved with alacrity.

As the reversed propeller of the starboard engine churned up the water in a turgid whirlpool, the *Stella* lost way rapidly. But not all her forward speed could be arrested at once. She still crabbed on towards the Casquets.

James Parton, passenger manager of a firm of shipowners, pale and morose, looked up from his book to see a great mass of rock towering by on the port beam. He could almost have leaned over the port rail and touched it. He recognised it as the Auquiere, the most westerly of the main rocks of the Casquet group. There was only one rock to the right of them, an insignificant one, the Black Rock, not more than 12 feet high. It looked as though the ship might escape. But he hurried below to get his wife. As he went he passed groups of agitated people.

'What a superb piece of seamanship!'

'My God, but that was close.'

'Are we safe?'

Fear, astonishment and relief were the progressive emotions of the passengers. The captain, it seemed, had got them out of a tight corner. But on the bridge Captain Reeks knew that his ship was almost certainly doomed. He was quoting to himself the relevant paragraph from the Channel

Pilot. 'There is a sunken rock with only four feet of water midway between the Auquiere and the Black Rock. No vessel should attempt to pass between them.'

His vessel was so handy that he could turn her short of the Black Rock, which he could see ahead, but not of the ledges which surrounded it. He had no alternative but to maintain the turn to starboard, past the Black Rock and out to sea, hoping to find sufficient water beneath him. But he could see the water rippling over the sunken rocks as he tried to avoid them. He waited for the vessel to strike.

When it came the shock was similar to the sudden braking of an express train. There was a rasping, scraping sound beneath the ship as the keel was ripped open, and the whole ship shuddered under the impact. The vessel seemed to take three distinct leaps as she struck first one submerged rock and then another. Passengers who were on their feet were thrown to the deck. In the ladies cabin, schoolteacher Annie Drake was thrown into the opposite berth. People rushed out of the saloons just in time to hear a shouted order from the bridge.

'Stand by to lower the boats.'

Captain Reeks turned to Wade and Reynolds. 'Hurry up and get the boats out. See that all the passengers have lifebelts.' They hurried from the bridge to supervise the work of the crew.

The time was four o'clock. The *Stella* should have been well short of the Casquets. Unaccountably, Captain Reeks had overrun his distance.

Water was already ankle-deep in the engine room, and the aft part of the ship was flooded. 'Close the water-tight doors!' ordered chief engineer Love. 'Let the steam out of the boilers!' He didn't want an engine-room explosion as the ship went down. As soon as he had given these orders he reported the situation to Captain Reeks on the speaking tube. 'Nothing can save her,' he told Reeks, 'she's been ripped open from amidships to stern.'

'Lower the boats,' ordered Captain Reeks. 'Women and children first.' In appreciation of the second order, some of the male passengers raised a cheer.

There was plenty of commotion on board as the crew hurried to their boat stations on the boat deck and as passengers rushed up to the main deck from the cabins, or rushed below to look for relatives. But there was no panic. 'There's plenty of time,' called Wade. 'All will be got safely off.'

The Reverend G. W. Clutterbuck, dark-haired, with trimmed beard and pince-nez, rushed on deck carrying two Gladstone bags. He called to a steward. 'Put these in the boats, will you?'

'Better put yourself in, sir,' advised the steward. The Reverend Clutterbuck dropped his bags and hurried aft.

In the ladies' cabin, Mary Rogers and Ada Preston were helping their charges to tie their lifebelts and get down the gangway on the main deck. 'There's nothing to be nervous about,' said Mary Rogers. 'There's room for all in the boats.' Many of the passengers, indeed, seemed unable to grasp their peril, and the cool behaviour of the crew almost convinced them that the ship was going to float. It wasn't until they saw a party of stokers rush up from the bowels of the ship and don lifebelts that passengers could be even half-convinced of their plight. Many unaccompanied women seemed rooted where they stood, unaware of their imminent danger.

When Reynolds reached the boat deck he made first for the port lifeboat. He was about to lower it, and the cook had got in, when he saw a group of passengers struggling with the starboard lifeboat and he went across to help. As a result, this was the first boat to be lowered and launched. The crew of four included Hartup, the look-out.

Stewards and male passengers formed a circle round the gangway, through which the women and children were passed one by one. Most of the women had to be forced to leave, and there were many tearful good-byes. The Reverend C. H. Bailey took his wife to the steps leading down to the boat, kissed her and told her to get in. To avoid the terrible temptation of trying to follow her he had to turn his back and walk away. One man did try to follow his wife but was restrained by the crew.

Chief Officer Wade was in his shirt-sleeves on the main deck organising passengers and crew. His wife Lillian, about to get into one of the boats, begged him to come with her. 'Now, Lill,' he said, 'never mind me. You know I can't leave the ship till everyone's off.' As she turned to move away from the boat he forced her back in. 'What you've got to do is think of the children.'

The party from Godalming, led by Alderman Collier, prepared themselves as best they could. The men strapped a lifejacket on Ethel Moon and persuaded her into the dinghy, which was now being launched. 'Ethel,' said Alderman Collier, 'we're on the Casquets. We shan't leave until all the women are safe. But I must order you to go.' Reluctantly she got into the dinghy.

Just before the dinghy left a man came forward with his wife and $3\frac{1}{2}$-year-old son, the youngest child on board. The man's name was Attwood, partner in a long-established Southampton furnishing business. He had to force his wife into the boat. She fell in and was caught by a seaman. Ethel Moon grabbed the boy.

When James Parton returned to the main deck with his wife the starboard lifeboat had gone and the dinghy was leaving. Mrs. Parton was the last person to get into the dinghy. Within a minute Parton saw a third boat being lowered from the same side—it was the starboard cutter. But meanwhile the *Stella* was settling with frightening rapidity. On the bridge Captain Reeks could see that the weight of water astern was tugging her down, dragging her off the ledge into deep water. There was only one more order he could give.

'Every man for himself! Do the best you can!'

The men needed no second bidding. Discipline so far had been good, but now, while many women still stood rooted to the deck, a swarm of men rushed forward to the starboard cutter.

Ernest Little, a naturalist, hadn't been able to persuade his wife to leave him. He dragged her to the cutter. 'If you don't get in this one,' he shouted, 'you won't get off at all. Jump!' As he spoke he pushed her and she fell headlong into the boat. When he saw the rush of men he jumped in after her.

A group of women were still huddled together astern. Many of the men who rushed for this boat did not even see them. James Parton, on the promenade deck, thought all the women had gone. He grabbed hold of a davit and slid down a rope into the cutter.

As the cutter pulled away, three women rushed to the starboard gangway on the main deck. They were intercepted by Chief Officer Wade. 'Ladies,' he told them calmly, 'your boat is on the other side.' Reynolds was now launching the port cutter.

Mary Rogers and Ada Preston had fitted lifebelts on all the women, but both were still on deck. As the port cutter was lowered, a woman came up from below without a lifebelt.

'Here—take mine,' said Mary Rogers.

'No, no—I shan't do that.'

'You shall, you shall—I'll get another.' And Mary Rogers took off her belt, fixed it securely round the woman's body, and hurried her to the port cutter, which was already full. The sailors squeezed her in.

'Jump in, Mrs. Rogers,' shouted the seamen.

'No—if I do I'll sink the boat. You're overloaded already. Good-bye. Good-bye.'

It was five minutes since the *Stella* had struck. Four boats with about a hundred people had got away, and the last lifeboat was about to be launched. If the *Stella* would only float for five more minutes there would be time to launch the two collapsible Berthon lifeboats from the boat deck and everyone would be saved.

Up on the boat deck, seamen were freeing the collapsible boats while Reynolds, helped by painter Edgar Anderson, solicitor Holland de Vesian, fireman George Lawrence and stoker Tom Buckley, launched the port lifeboat. Norman, the cook, was still sitting inside.

Among the passengers waiting for the launching were Mrs. Arnold and her sons Bening and Claude. While she waited, Mrs. Arnold pinned the discarded football to her elder son's coat to help him stay afloat, at the same time resolving to hold on to her younger son herself.

The Reverend Clutterbuck, his Gladstone bags forgotten but still wearing his pince-nez, no longer seemed a figure of fun. He was on his knees in the stern of the ship with the women, praying with them, urging them to make for the boats.

Captain Reeks was on the bridge. So were seamen Johnson and Davey, both of whom refused to leave him.

The *Stella* was slipping off the rocks. Her stern was already under water, her bows were lifting. Nearly a hundred people were still on board. Captain Reeks, standing at attention, was forced to grab the rail to save himself from being thrown backwards. He shouted down at the boats, which were still perilously near the ship. 'For the love of God keep clear.'

The Reverend Clutterbuck, still on his knees with the women, was swept with them into the sea, then dragged down with them as the stern sank in deep water. As the bows lifted slowly towards the vertical, the removal van broke adrift from its lashings, rolled on to its side and crashed through the rails in a cloud of foam. Captain Reeks still clung to the bridge, still somehow an erect, commanding figure.

For those amidships it seemed that everything solid and dependable was suddenly receding beneath them. The water rose in giant walls around the ship as though it would crush her, then folded inwards and broke over her with tidal impact, forcing her down to the lowest depths.

The people in the boats, some no more than 20 yards away, heard the tremendous roar of tumbling water and the hiss of suction and steam as the vessel went down. Scores of people jumped off the decks into the water and scores more were dragged under as she went. The *Stella* had gone down in six minutes. The port lifeboat had not been launched, nor had either of the Berthon collapsible boats.

Fear of being drawn into the vortex of the sinking ship was quickly supplanted, in the boats, by fear of being capsized by the rush of desperate swimmers who dived off the *Stella* as she sank. All the good swimmers made straight for the boats. Only the first to reach them got in. Edward Abinger was one of them. He had had time to take off his greatcoat before jumping in. He finished up in the starboard cutter.

Many of the swimmers grabbed at gunwales that were already almost awash and were pushed away by the oarsmen. Women sitting at the side of the boats were seized by the arm in urgent appeal. Drowning men were unceremoniously dissuaded from further entreaty by a blow with the flat of an oar.

It was a nightmare scene as the four overladen boats tried desperately to pull away and stay afloat. The pantechnicon van had floated clear and a crowd of men and women were clutching the sides and a few were sitting on the roof. People were clinging to rafts and wreckage, many of them were shouting and screaming for help. There was nothing that anyone in the lifeboats could do for them, except fend them off if they succeeded in getting too close. Bodies were strewn like litter everywhere, many still wearing lifebelts which had slipped and forced faces under water and legs grotesquely into the air. For an hour the scene around the hidden wreck was a kaleidoscope of drama and tragedy, until the currents around the rocks and the efforts of the oarmen dispersed the boats, and the human litter began to clear as numbed fingers released their tenuous hold on life.

The men who had been trying to launch the port lifeboat all went under with the ship. Most of them floated to the surface afterwards and swam to rafts or bits of wreckage. George Reynolds, the second mate, miraculously reached the starboard lifeboat and was taken aboard. He was the only officer saved. Captain Reeks, First Officer Wade and all the engineers went down with the ship.

Apart from Ethel Moon, all Alderman Collier's party were lost. Dr. Philip Davis, too, was unable to keep his promise to follow his friend Mrs. Aylett in a later boat. Allen and his wife were saved.

Holland de Vesian struck his head against something as he neared the surface and was conscious of an enveloping darkness. It was some time before it occurred to him that he was trapped under an upturned boat. It was the port lifeboat, which had floated clear. He managed to crawl out and clamber on top, where he was joined by the cook. The cook had been sitting in the boat when the ship went down; he had broken both legs.

Others who swam to the upturned boat were the painter Anderson, fireman Buckley, stoker Lawrence, and seaman Johnson, the man who had been at the wheel when the ship struck and who had stayed on the bridge with the captain. There was no sign of Davey.

Another passenger who came to the surface, helped by the buoyancy of a football, was the lad Bening Arnold. Conscience-stricken at the loss of his mother and brother, who had drowned beside him, he made no effort at first to save himself. He was dragged on to the upturned port lifeboat by Anderson.

Soon there were 14 people clinging to this upturned boat. They were still there two hours later when darkness fell. But during the night the boat heeled over and righted itself, throwing the clinging survivors into the sea. In the darkness and confusion two men disappeared. One of them was the injured cook. The plug of the boat was missing and it filled at once with water. The gunwales were practically submerged and only the two air compartments kept it afloat. Seaman Johnson rowed hour after hour up to his waist in water, fighting to keep the boat off the rocks.

The people in the other boats were also struggling to keep off the rocks. Many of the men passengers took a turn at the oars—and so did some of the women. Greta Williams and her sister Theresa were in the dinghy. Some of the boat's occupants, cold and seasick, weak from immersion and exposure, prayed for death. Greta Williams whispered to her sister. 'Theresa—would you like me to sing?'

'Do you think you can?'

'I can try.'

Thus it was that the contralto voice of a famous concert singer drifted with pellucid clarity across the treacherous currents of the Casquets, reaching at least one more of the boats. It was not a steady voice, far from it, and the song chosen was a hymn, but the imploring, heartfelt melody proved deeply comforting, expressing as it did the hope of delivery when daylight came.

All the people in the four boats that had been successfully launched survived the night. But there were further casualties in the waterlogged port lifeboat. One of the ship's firemen, who had been badly burned by escaping steam, died and was pushed overboard. Able Seaman Johnson, who never once complained, rowed until he literally dropped dead. Quite suddenly he threw up his arms, let out a strangled cry, and collapsed over the oar. Holland de Vesian nursed him for several minutes in vain. He too was put overboard.

A third man died, and then a fourth. No one had the strength to lift the fourth man over the gunwale and his body slopped about the boat for the rest of the night. When morning came, of the original 14 who had clambered on to the upturned boat only 8 remained.

Still no one knew of the tragedy. Nothing had been heard on the Casquets except a suspicion of a sound that it was thought might be voices and a noise as of a ship blowing off steam.

The *Ibex* arrived in Guernsey 90 minutes late and reported fog in the Casquets area. Friends waiting to meet the *Stella* assumed that the captain had decided to lie off the Casquets until daylight. It was not until Good Friday morning that the *Vera*, another South Western steamer, picked up the first of the *Stella*'s boats. By that time the people clinging to wreckage or the pantechnicon van had long since succumbed to exposure. But all five boats were picked up during the day.

There were pathetic scenes at Guernsey when women parted from their husbands peered for them amongst the remaining survivors, mostly in vain. Joyous reunions were few. Yet 119 people were saved—a remarkable number considering the speed with which the *Stella* went down. The exact number of passengers who sailed from Southampton that Thursday morning was never established, but about 70 people were known to be missing.

The enquiry set up into the disaster found that Captain Reeks had erred in not stopping his ship short of the Casquets to take soundings before proceeding at slow speed. No one who knew Reeks could believe that he would knowingly have hazarded his ship, yet he seemed to have acted recklessly and to have run full tilt into the very dangers it was his duty to avoid.

How much his judgment was affected by the parallel sailing of the *Ibex* was hotly argued at the time. The enquiry pointed to the timing of the two services as being unwise and inviting trouble, but the court lacked the courage to find that there had in fact been racing. The fairest conclusion may be

that Captain Reeks overran his distance through some unex-
plained phenomenon of tide and current, but that in the
foggy conditions he would not have been steaming at full
speed but for the *Ibex*.

By his behaviour at the finish Captain Reeks was ad-
judged—in the sentiment of the times—to have redeemed
himself and cleared his name. His end had been heroic. But
the people took to their hearts not a hero but a heroine, one
whose duties were humble but who, like her captain,
sacrificed her life for others and went down with the ship.
Today, more than 70 years later, a memorial fountain still
stands on the Western Esplanade at Southampton, recalling
the story of Mary Rogers, stewardess of the *Stella*, and her
wonderful steadfastness in the confusion and terror of shipwreck.

* * *

While I was working on this story I learned of the
death of the internationally-known contralto Grace
Williams at the age of 95. But I did in fact find one
survivor—Jack Attwood, who, as a $3\frac{1}{2}$-year-old boy,
had been the youngest passenger on board. He retains
vivid memories of the disaster, and remembers particularly the moment of parting between his mother
and father, and later looking back at the *Stella* 'bow
high in the air, stern down on the rocks', just before she
sank. The experience did not deter him from qualify-
ing as an engineer and spending his life at sea—mostly
on the Channel Islands run.

The wife of one seaman lost in the disaster, Tom
Glover, was killed by a horse-drawn van in East Street,
Southampton at just about the time the *Stella* went
down, so neither knew of the other's fate. The wife was
thus spared the revelation that her husband had left
another widow and family in Jersey.